PARADOXES OF ORDER

ROBERT K. MORRIS

PARADOXES OF ORDER

SOME PERSPECTIVES ON THE FICTION
OF V. S. NAIPAUL

A LITERARY FRONTIERS EDITION
UNIVERSITY OF MISSOURI PRESS
COLUMBIA

Excerpts from *An Area of Darkness* have been reprinted by permission of Andre Deutsch, Limited, Copyright © 1964 by V. S. Naipaul, and Macmillan Publishing Co., Inc., Copyright © 1965 by V. S. Naipaul.

Excerpts from *The Mimic Men* have been reprinted by permission of Andre Deutsch, Limited, and Macmillan Publishing Co., Inc., Copyright © 1967 by V. S. Naipaul.

Acknowledgment is made to Andre Deutsch, Limited, and Alfred A. Knopf, Inc., for permission to quote from *In a Free State* by V. S. Naipaul. Copyright © 1971 by V. S. Naipaul.

John Cushman Associates, Inc., has granted permission to quote from *A Flag on the Island*, Copyright © 1967 and 1968 by V. S. Naipaul; *Mr Stone and the Knights Companion*, Copyright © 1963 by V. S. Naipaul; and *A House for Mr Biswas*, Copyright © 1963 by V. S. Naipaul.

ISBN 0–8262–0172–5
Library of Congress Catalog Card Number 74–23752
Printed and bound in the United States of America
Copyright © 1975 by
The Curators of the University of Missouri
Columbia, Missouri
All rights reserved

Library of Congress Cataloging in Publication Data
Morris, Robert K
    Paradoxes of order.

    (A Literary frontiers edition)
    Includes bibliographical references.
    1. Naipaul, Vidiadhar Surajprasad—Criticism and interpretation. I. Title.
PR9272.9N32Z77   823   74–23752
ISBN 0–8262–0172–5

FOR RON AND JULIE PEIERLS

PARADOXES OF ORDER

IN the long title story of a collection published in 1967 when Vidiadhar Surajprasad Naipaul was thirty-five, "A Flag on the Island," a middle-aged American, Frankie, returns to the spot in the Caribbean where he had served as a GI during World War II. He finds it drastically changed. Instead of the Union Jack or the Stars and Stripes, a new flag—"rays from the yellow sun lighting up a wavy blue sea"—now flies. The small, shabby but intimate bar he once knew as "Henry's place" has been transformed into The Coconut Grove, an expensive and garish tourist trap: its name advertised everywhere by publicity flyers and splashed grossly on billboards. An old acquaintance, H. J. Blackwhite, who taught skills at a business school and churned out unsellable romantic novels in his spare time, has become a popular black novelist. Gary Priest, an inept insurance salesman, appears nightly on television as Gary Priestland, a talk-show/revivalist czar. And Selma, a free and irresponsible spirit who haunted Henry's place and eventually became Frankie's mistress, is now Mrs. Priestland, moving in bourgeois boredom between refrigerator and Mixmaster.

At first Frankie feels that the changes on the island have occurred independently of his own; but little by little he acknowledges that he cannot, sensibly, relive the past, that "all landscapes are, in the end, only in the imagination; to be faced with the reality is to start again." Yet as the reality of the present arrays itself in neat, grim, shocking little ways, Frankie comes to see that the "world is being washed away" for him as well as for the island; not only has he become caught up in the change, but in some measure he has been responsible for it. His well-meaning attempts to alter the do-nothing and disorderly lives of his friends, to impress upon them the values of a go-getter, have come home to roost with a vengeance. The vitality they had communicated because they lacked sophistication and ambition has been numbed by a world-weariness ripe for Armageddon:

> "Sometimes [Henry tells Frankie] you want the world to end. You can't go back and do things again. They begin just like that, they get good. The only thing is you never know they good until they finish. I wish the hurricane would come and blow away all this. I feel the world need this sort of thing every now then. A clean break, a fresh start. But the damn world don't end. And we don't dead at the right time."[1]

What Frankie at last realizes is that the patina of commercialism cannot hide the cracks and flaws of personality that run through him, as well as through his old friends. Time, the modern shape of things, but no less his interference and exploitive "frankness" have turned individualists into pandering, corrupted, materialistic monsters of success.

Though overshadowed by the enormous energy and cultural sweep of Naipaul's second-best novel to come out of his Caribbean background (*A House for Mr Biswas*) and the moral and political range of his best novel (*The Mimic Men*), "A Flag on the Island," though I do not discuss it in detail here, is a remarkable novella. By "remarkable" I do not allude to its necessarily being amenable to varieties of explication, but rather to its holding in balance—perhaps to a finer degree than any of his longer works—what is of perma-

---

1. *A Flag on the Island* (Baltimore, 1969), p. 191.

nent interest about him, his style and the themes of his fiction.

As for the first of these, the man. Those familiar with but the broadest outlines of Naipaul's life will detect certain similarities between Frankie's impressions of his changed fun-island-in-the-sun and Naipaul's own testament of return to Trinidad as recounted some years earlier in *The Middle Passage* (1962). And while one would hardly care to connect the biography of the author's surrogate (American, ex-GI and ex-hot-shot, businessman) with the author himself (grandson of an indentured laborer who came to Trinidad from India, Caribbean-born, Oxford-educated, lapsed Hindu, renowned writer), they share an attitude that goes beyond the confines of antecedents or patrimonies. The attitude in question is central to life and to art and tells us a good deal more about Naipaul's personal and creative intelligence than most stories narrated in the first person are (owing to the built-in technical and esthetic peculiarities of the form) generally allowed to do.

I am referring to Frankie's observation quoted above that "all landscapes are, in the end, only in the imagination; to be faced with the reality is to start again." The line is crucial to "A Flag on the Island" but no less pertinent to the rest of the Naipaul canon and to the sensibility that informs it. Frankie—and Naipaul—dwells on the changed and changing landscape not as disappointed tourist (or even disappointed lover) lapsed into nostalgia and sentiment, but as one who acknowledges how something once stable and meaningful has shown itself to be impermanent and meaningless. Naipaul confesses in his chapter on Trinidad in *The Middle Passage* that he "felt all [the] old fear" on first returning to the country of his birth: a reaction prompted by his recalling what it might have been like for him had he remained there. And to note how vastly different in tone and feeling a book like *The Middle Passage* is from the earlier novels is to sense how Frankie's observation, so immediate and personal, can, mediated by art, give rise to no less than a world outlook.

Being a "remembrance of things past," "A Flag on the Island" has Proustian, and consequently "artistic" overtones. Yet the sharp, necessary division Naipaul willingly makes between the real and imagined, the literal and symbolic extends into provinces other than art. Much of Naipaul's originality comes from his ability to relate the "universal human predicament"[2] to the substance of place, as well as to its spirit. The reason Naipaul's sense of place is paramount in his books should become clearer once we understand that since leaving Trinidad at eighteen, he has "belonged" nowhere. Naipaul is in league with other modern expatriates who (because they are expatriates, with no fixed abode) must gain a fix on reality through their art. Landscapes are for Naipaul what Dublin was for Joyce, what Manicheanism is for Burgess, what baroque acrostics are for Nabokov: symbolic and metaphorical structures built upon very real feelings of rootlessness and expatriation.

From his first major novel, *A House for Mr Biswas*, landscapes—rendered with the eye of one who has been intimate with them momentarily, has consigned them to the imagination, and is intimate with them no longer—have figured prominently in Naipaul's work. Mr. Biswas' Trinidad, the very different

2. Louis James in *Contemporary Novelists* (New York, 1972), p. 921.

Trinidad of Ralph Singh (*The Mimic Men*) and his London, the still-different London of Mr. Stone and his London suburbs, and the endless and changing stretches of road in the Africa of "In a Free State" show a hypersensitivity to place that one does not frequently find in writers who take their native ground for granted. Perhaps to the expatriate artist, who is always homeless and always at home, every place must be encountered again as though it had never been encountered before. This is the world outlook I associate with Naipaul, and the objectivity and sympathy of the man combine further to create the singular fusion of reality and imagination that characterizes him as an artist.

How this feeling and intelligence are linked to style can be briefly illustrated by some paragraphs toward the end of "A Flag on the Island." They describe the island on the day after a hurricane:

> Morning, dark and turbulent, revealed the full dereliction of the beach. Fishing boats reclined or were propped up on the sand that was still golden. . . [but] scuffed and marked and bloody like an arena; it was littered with the heads and entrails of fish. Mangy pariah dogs, all rib and bone, all bleached to a nondescript fawn colour, moved listlesly, their tails between their legs, from [oil] drum to yellow drum. Black vultures weighed down the branches of coconut trees; some hopped awkwardly on the sand; many more circled overhead.
>
> We drove back to the city. . . under a low dark sky. It was early, yet the island was alive. The streets were full of people. . . . All normal activity had been suspended. It was like a continuation of the night before; the streets were even more like aquaria, thick with life, but silent. Only the absence of the blackness of night seemed to have marked the passage of time. . . .

> Then it was night again.... Against the black sky blacker points moved endlessly: all the birds of the island, flying south. It was like the final abandonment. (pp. 210–11)

I perhaps need not stress how the outlines of the hurricane's aftermath are made more "real"[3] by being backlit by certain eccentricities of imagination that, not necessarily in themselves but in the author's projection of them into the mind of his protagonist, are patently "unreal." The "blurring of fantasy and reality" that induces in Frankie "feelings of helplessness" becomes for Naipaul an artistic method and stylistic device—here and throughout all his novels—to turn the ordinary into the extraordinary without violating character or without undue editorializing.

The "realism" in these three paragraphs is achieved through a most logical spatial and temporal progression: the movement from seashore to city, from morning to night. What sustains the movement, however, is not mere logic, but intensity and continuity. The early morning and afternoon darkness gathers itself into the blackness of night, while the still boats, listless dogs, and minimally active vultures of the first paragraph give way to the pulsating and electric city of the second, and the almost infinite motion of the third. Added to this, Naipaul's studied concreteness (his emphasis on color) and his passion for flat, generally unemphatic description call attention to the

---

3. Being aware that all art is artifice, and that terms like *real, realistic, fantasy*, etc., beg some critical as well as stylistic questions, I have surrounded these terms with quotes. I beg to be excused for taking the easy way out. But to deviate into an esthetico-linguistico-literary argument as to whether such terms have a right to exist in literature or not, would severely complicate a rather straightforward analysis of Naipaul's art and style.

scene rather than to the language, locating it at a particular place and at a particular time.

And yet on rereading, the "fantastic" effects of the scene register more strongly than the "naturalistic" ones. Backtracking a bit, one notes a metaphysical (or metanatural) movement throughout: from inanimate (boats) to animal (dogs) to human (the people in the streets) to suprahuman (*all* the birds). What Naipaul is trying to convey is an ultimate participation in an act of nature as it changes in Frankie's mind from literal havoc (the dereliction on the beach) to a kind of apocalypse ("it was like the final abandonment").

That simile, no less than the spare seeding of others, is persuasive enough to carry us to fantasy without necessarily surrendering our hold on the former. The sand, likened to a bloody arena "littered with the heads and entrails of fish," is a remarkable simile in itself, but it becomes surcharged with a strange and additional meaning when, a few lines below, Naipaul likens the street to an "aquaria, thick with life, but silent." It is that sort of registering on the imagination that can allow a thunderstorm to permanently traumatize one of Naipaul's earlier protagonists, and the drowning of a total stranger to emotionally maim a later one.[4]

Like his similes, Naipaul's symbols fashion from reality what is bizarre and grotesque through maddeningly logical connections. The best example here is the linking of the brooding, hopping, circling vultures with the migrating birds. Each suggests the dereliction and abandonment connected both with Naipaul's view of the island and with Frankie; but where we initially relate these conditions of human vulnerability to death,

---

4. Mohun Biswas in *A House for Mr Biswas*; Ralph Singh in *The Mimic Men*.

we finally understand that Naipaul is relating them to life, and to Frankie's life in particular. Thus Naipaul sets out ostensibly to chart what is "real" about a ravaged landscape, and ends by mapping the "fantastic" shifts of a mind that, like the minds of us all, must order and interpret as best it can the countless, chaotic impressions it receives.

Here, if not exhaustively and complexly, then certainly directly, Naipaul shows the art and thought controlling the principal theme of his major novels and stories. All of his fiction is concerned in one way or another with the individual's attempt to order the world after his own view of it, and finally to discover how innocence is inevitably lost, how one's peculiar sense of order breaks down, and how the self may be falsified in the process. This perspective is admittedly not always cheerful and has become less so in the twenty years in which Naipaul has developed as a writer. But for all his skepticism and irony, it seems to me that he is one of the few novelists today—Doris Lessing is another—who has seen how possibly futile it may be to create any but a fragile vision of order amidst the normative chaos of our modern world.

To say that a Naipaul protagonist embarks on his quest for order out of the need to escape what has been fixed by the past, or out of the need to change the present, or—as most often is the case in the best of these novels—out of both needs together, should anticipate some of the larger dilemmas and conflicts he is certain to face. One contingency of escape, for example, is freedom; yet another is exile, the condition common to those defecting from their roots, origins, and culture. And as we read further in Naipaul we discover that such a condition is not uncommon in the least. Moreover, however static that world, caught in the vise of the past, may be, its familiar and predictable patterns spell out a kind of security; and however compelling the notion that change will conjure up a happier future, those invariable chance encounters with people who have quite different notions, and with forces that move them, show how change, as well as being attractive, can also be precarious and disillusioning. For the change predicated on mobility means the surrender of stability. Men like Mohun Biswas, Richard Stone, Ralph Singh, Bobby, Frankie are forced to choose freely between one state and the other, and like the fabled donkey equidistant from the two bales of hay they often vacillate between them. Yet choose they do. Goaded by their rejection of the past and lured by what they hope to find in the future, they struggle to realize a new scheme of order before they have shaken off the older one; and it is from this very movement, which may cover a day (*In A Free State*), a year (*Mr Stone and the Knights Companion*), more than twenty years (*The Mimic Men*), or a lifetime (*A House for Mr Biswas*), that the paradoxes of existence arise.

I am of course looking ahead to Naipaul's major works. In his earliest writing, the three books of the fifties set in and around Trinidad, the paradoxes generated by the quest for order are as yet undeveloped. In *Miguel Street*, the first book Naipaul wrote, though the third to be published, they are parceled out among the several dozen inhabitants of a slum street in Port of Spain whose characters sift through the consciousness of the young narrator: a street 'rab of rare sensitivity, intelligence and humanity, who is able to lend something poignant and profound to the malleable experiences of marginal lives.

Those living on Miguel Street seem, at first blush,

misfits or eccentrics. It is the simplest view to take of them, and in Naipaul's attempt to be both dispassionate and sympathetic, not an unreasonable one. Gradually, however, we are made aware that it is perhaps not the people who are out of kilter but life itself. The awareness imparts considerably more weight to these linked sketches and vignettes, because we are never really certain whether the amoral and eccentric are being presented with an air of normalcy, or whether the narrator—despite those qualities I mentioned above—is himself eccentric enough to make life, in its many bizarre contexts and attitudes, seem normal.

Yet the central paradox of *Miguel Street* is not that the narrator senses any particular order in these lives governed by poverty, frustration, aborted ambition, boredom, defeat, ignorance, cruelty, deception, drunkenness, and superstition, but that the characters themselves do. "Life a helluva thing," says Hat, one of the great originals in the book. "You can see trouble coming and you can't do a damn thing to prevent it coming. You just got to sit and watch and wait" (*Miguel Street*, Penguin Books, 1958, p. 91). Ironically, the vitality and fervor of Hat, and those like him, come from this stoic view of life that the narrator finally eschews in leaving the island. For those who remain, throbbing with disorder, dreams, fantasies, the street really gives the only order they know. And they embark on their imaginary flights to escape with the understanding that they can return to the safety of Miguel Street should they fail, as they always do. It is, if I may amplify the paradox, the orderly disorderliness that imparts coherence to the world of Miguel Street, trapped by its own freedom and license. "The final fraudulence," Frankie is to say ten years later, "we cannot avoid; we might look for escape, but we are always careful to provide for escape from that escape."

In some ways *Miguel Street* might be taken as a Caribbean *Winesburg, Ohio*, though unlike Anderson's novel it is a finger exercise rather than a work of maturity. They share an essential concentration on a microcosm that establishes homogeneity of place and theme from heterogeneity of character. And it shows how the concentrated futility of lives can give "ordinary" eccentrics a vitality far beyond those who lead normal, or continual, lives. *Miguel Street* orders a world where the dream of escape and change seems straightforward enough, but where the capricious and erratic movement toward the goal only emphasizes how chaotic the lives really are. Between the dream and the goal Naipaul's zany characters display themselves with reckless brilliance, even though they all settle back into the common slough of despond and despair. The text for *Miguel Street*, as for Naipaul's two subsequent novels, might have come, once we are keyed in to the energy set in motion by humming disorder, from still another American, Henry Adams, who wrote in his *Education* that "chaos often breeds life, when order breeds habit."

This most exacting truth is at the core of *The Mystic Masseur* and *The Suffrage of Elvira*, both of which pose the paradox that early marked Naipaul as being nothing if not cynical and detached about his birthplace. For in them the everyday teeming, breeding, heterogeneous, pullulating world of Trinidad breaks down into an order that homogenizes their two nominal heroes into—Naipaul was later to use the phrase as the title of his finest novel—"mimic men." Ganesh Ramsumair of the first, and Surujpat ("Pat") Harbans of the second do manage change, do engineer, after much frustration and an equal amount of luck, a questionable order. But to what end these comic originals and their rich and varied antic dance emerge as faceless puppets jerked along in a political charade remains more questionable still.

The theme central to these two novels is actually historical—subjectively historical—and some years after they were written, when Naipaul revisited Trinidad on a commission to write a book about the Caribbean, he spelled it out:

> I had never examined [my] fear of Trinidad. I had never wished to. In my novels I had only expressed this fear; and it is only now, at the moment of writing, that I am able to attempt to examine it. I knew Trinidad to be unimportant, uncreative, cynical. . . . Power was recognized, but dignity was allowed to no one. Every person of eminence was held to be crooked and contemptible. We lived in a society which denied itself heroes.
>
> It was a place where the stories were never stories of success but of failure. . . .
>
> It was also a place where a recurring word of abuse was "conceited", an expression of the resentment felt of anyone who possessed unusual skills. Such skills were not required by a society which produced nothing, never had to prove its worth, and was never called upon to be efficient.[5]

Given these circumstances and attitudes, it would seem that anyone with a bit of ambition or vision would stay on, unless he were a fool or a masochist. Yet whatever solid conclusions Naipaul drew after his return to Trinidad were scarcely made so monochromatic in the earlier fiction. I find it hard to read either of these novels without sensing Naipaul's strongly ambivalent feelings about Ganesh and Surujpat: those little, unsophisticated men, pretentious and aspiring, trapped

---

5. *The Middle Passage* (Baltimore, 1959), pp. 43–45.

by the disorder of their culture and spurred on by itching egos, who try to dig out from the debris of a stagnant society. "Heroes" they are, and something more; but in becoming "heroes," something less.

Naipaul describes the degree of disorder with oblique understatement in one of the early chapters of *The Suffrage of Elvira*:

> Things were crazily mixed up in Elvira. Everybody, Hindus Muslims and Christians, owned a Bible; the Hindus and Muslims looking on it, if anything, with greater awe. Hindus and Moslems celebrated Christmas and Easter. The Spaniards and some of the Negroes celebrated the Hindu festival of lights.... Everybody celebrated the Muslim festival of Hosein. In fact, when Elvira was done with religious festivals, there were few straight days left.[6]

In *The Suffrage of Elvira* the charm of this "crazily mixed up" interculturation withers before its stagnancy and inefficiency. In *The Mystic Masseur*, Naipaul, obliquely again, shows how cultural disorder and the exigencies of a melting-pot society make demands even on one so tolerant and charitable and likable as Ganesh, who, at the height of his powers as a rich and respected mystic, cannot quite see how his universalizing instincts lay the groundwork for his ultimate fraudulence:

> He was no bigot. Ht took as much interest in Christianity and Islam as in Hinduism. In the shrine, the old bedroom, he had pictures of Mary and Jesus next to Krishna and Vishnu; a crescent and star represented iconoclastic Islam. "All the same God," he said.[7]

When Ganesh's pictures are overshadowed by signs of self-advertisement (in Hindi and English) and when

6. *The Suffrage of Elvira* (Baltimore, 1969), p. 66.
7. *The Mystic Masseur* (Baltimore, 1969), p. 139.

the toilet roll in his lavatory plays "Yankee Doodle Dandy" whenever the paper is pulled, his transformation—and his surrender to cultural bastardization—is almost complete. It is not the least of the ironies in *The Mystic Masseur* that Ganesh falls from love and respect when he fails to pacify and unite demonstrating strikers. Ganesh is done in by disorder.

The Suffrage of Elvira and *The Mystic Masseur* generate their comedy from the disordered world of Trinidad. Yet in the end they cannot strictly be called comic novels. Naipaul's ambivalence about Trinidad comes through with marked cynicism, and a nod to the theme central to the novels may explain why. Both are broadly concerned with the success of the little man. In the one, the effete, naive, autodidact Ganesh Ramsumair mounts, through a concatenation of chance, island superstition (*obeah*), and corruption to become first a popular masseur, then a mystic, writer, pundit, politico, and finally a representative in the assembly. Inevitably, Ganesh exchanges his constituency and title of M.L.C. (Member of the Legislative Council) for an M.B.E. (Member of the British Empire), loses his status as cult figure and hero of the people, is mocked in calypsos, and even, capping his progress, anglicizes his name to G. Ramsay Muir. In *The Suffrage of Elvira*, Surujpat Harbans' shaky course to the legislative council careers through the comic intrigue, boondoggling, and logrolling attending democracy's rise in Trinidad and its first general election. "Pat" totally sells out in order to win the seat and in winning, disowns all those factions that helped him—Hindu, Moslem, black—surrendering honesty, innocence, and wonder to the fascination for the power that transports him from Trinidad's backward counties to Port of Spain.

The novels convert *Miquel Street*'s abortive

dreams of success into realities, but at a cost that bankrupts ethics and personality. Ganesh and Surujpat unshackle themselves from their imprisoning ambience only by severing links with their culture. If they win new identities, it is by losing the value, originality, vitality of their old selves. No one, the little man least of all, can resist that first taste of power and prosperity that nourishes the starved ego. And ego—the thinking, feeling, acting self—is as fine and solid a grip as one can get on life, far more substantial than the airier handles of honor and friendship. But as Naipaul's cool, cumulative ironies make clear, success bought at the expense of spirit and through an evasion that means fraudulence and betrayal must count—paradoxically—as the grandest of failures. The snobbism of the turncoats who succeed sounds the prelude to a cultural isolation far more damaging than the insulation of those who fail. Success means completing the vision of order to escape from disorder; but what price success?

The pose of those Trinidadians who "make it" is—if we pay close enough attention to what Naipaul says in *The Middle Passage*—relatively simple to understand; the position, however, is a bit more complex, and perhaps only one who has personally experienced the subtle shifts accruing from severance, reorientation, and change can analyze it. Naipaul has. He may well be the first contemporary to penetrate the psyche of the British colonial minority cultures by tunneling outward from the core. Compare Naipaul on Trinidad with Forster on India, Orwell on Burma, Burgess on Malaya to see how the Englishman's exploration of interior regions, however compassionate, sensitive, or intelligent, retains the anxiety and guilt of the white man's failure to strike a rapprochement between British and colonial cultures. Naipaul, as he develops from

Miguel Street to *The Mimic Men*, is far more objective, even harsh, in writing about the disparity, far more willing to relieve the white man of the white man's burden and to recognize that in his urgent desire, his necessity to dispense with the substance of the older, indigenous culture, the minority colonial who would succeed had little choice but to ape the mere forms of his adopted culture.

Unhappily, the lengthening shadow of modernism and the retreating shadow of Empire fell over Trinidad at much the same time in history, during and immediately after World War II. The Trinidadian Hindu's relationship to his two cultures, previously only ambivalent (as I have suggested was Naipaul's own case) became paradoxical. Naipaul records in *An Area of Darkness*:

> To see the culture of my childhood as the result of a dramatic confrontation of opposed worlds would be to distort the reality. To me the worlds were juxtaposed and mutually exclusive. One gradually contracted. It had to; it fed only on memories and its completeness was only apparent. It was yielding not to attack but to a type of seepage from the other.[8]

Consequently, the success that came from championing the new could only be realized through an osmotic drain on the old; no synthesis of cultures was possible. The baby, alas, was thrown out with the bath water; but whether into the Caribbean or the Channel made very little difference—least of all, I suspect, to the baby! Thus, for Ganesh and Surujpat, the jettisoning of the older values and their imperfect and illusive re-

---

8. *An Area of Darkness* (Baltimore, 1968), p. 35. Naipaul is here discussing the peculiar relationship of the Trinidadian Hindu to his culture; like Naipaul, Ganesh and Surrujpat are both Hindus.

placement of them by newer ones meant concession to the paradox. And in achieving success at the expense of moral and ethical authenticity, which, if he were to succeed, had to be rejected, the new political man aggravated, rather than inflamed, the confusions and divisions within the jumble that was Trinidad.

Miguel Street, *The Mystic Masseur*, and *The Suffrage of Elvira* show Trinidad falling between the two stools, which were themselves to be kicked over in *A House for Mr Biswas* and *The Mimic Men*. As social comedies whose comedy and plot outweigh social content and character, the early novels cannot pretend to rival in art the subsequent epics. But as blueprints for roughing out the details Naipaul was to fill in when constructing the various worlds of his more mature works, they are of considerable importance. Naipaul has emerged as one of the most thoughtful writers of the postwar period because of his shifting and challenging views on at least one great problem fundamental to our age. But his originality, indeed his complexity, are found not merely in his willingness to explore this theme of order from longitude to longitude, but to move outward, with impressive scope and freedom and risk, to the latitudes.

This critique is an attempt to study this movement and theme much as they developed over Naipaul's twenty years' progress as expatriate, novelist, thinker, self-imposed exile. Its thesis is contained in, though I hope not confined to, its title; and its title is to serve as a solid foundation for some close, and perhaps often quirky readings on ideas that have obsessed Naipaul, me, and, I should not be at all surprised, most contemporaries who have grown up with and pondered them. Like Naipaul's many books, this one small book of observation and interpretation tries to follow ideas of order (a literary theme as well as a major metaphor of life) from their simplest statement through their profound, and in some ways terrifying development. Since Naipaul is still a very active and flourishing writer, no coda is forthcoming. What I offer here in criticism is what Naipaul has orchestrated in his fiction: vertical variations on a horizontal theme. Hopefully they will prove interesting in themselves; more hopefully, they may illuminate paradoxes not only central to a writer and his work, but to our times and within ourselves.

M. BISWAS, ARCHITECT OF ORDER

> Everything which made the Indian alien in the society gave him strength.... His religion gave him values which were not the white values of the rest of the community, and preserved him from self contempt; he never lost pride in his origins. More important than religion was his family organization, an enclosing self-sufficient world absorbed with its quarrels and jealousies, as difficult for the outsider to penetrate as for one of its members to escape. It protected and imprisoned, a static world, awaiting decay.[1]

ONE may accept Naipaul's expatriate detachment more readily than his hard-core cynicism in his first three Caribbean novels. His geographical isolation from Trinidad, his tough mindedness toward the cultural and social muddle, his long-range, dead-center focus on the potential truths and distortions of character

1. *The Middle Passage* (Baltimore, 1969), p. 88.

account for both attitudes. But where in other expatriate writers distance might have the affect of composing modulations into nostalgia and involvement, with Naipaul it prompted only a stoney, impassive, unrelieved objectivity.

One cause for this attitude was his feeling of never having really belonged to the Caribbean culture to begin with; another was his transplantation to an England whose culture he had absorbed but which he was now only beginning to experience first hand. Feeling like an exile in Trinidad, Naipaul suffered the emotional displacement that often breeds inarticulateness or alienation. As a Trinidadian in self-imposed exile and an aspiring writer given to coherency, he needed to convert the emotional into an intellectual response, to articulate what were fundamentally the means and ends of this displacement: in other words, to preserve in fiction what he considered a moribund society and lay its ghosts to rest.

I realize this interpretation may hint at the biographical heresy in criticism, though I hope I will be acquitted of any psychoanalyzing. The fact is that in these early novels the cynic in Naipaul—who was not yet thirty—outdistances the satirist and ironist. It would seem almost impossible to be surrounded by a sea of material and not completely immersed in it; yet Naipaul seems to be just that. He touches Trinidad at all of its sensitive points, but without any feeling, as thought its people, who directly inspired him, are the untouchables and great unwashed from whom he is finally content to be removed. The writer (it is a bit tricky now to talk about the man) seems secure in his own intellectual sufficiency; though displaced from his home and his material, he is happily and safely displaced.

I am not questioning here the justness or rightness of Naipaul's tone so much as analyzing its literary effectiveness. Since he was to question it himself in his major novel on Trinidad, *A House for Mr Biswas*, indeed to drastically shift tone because of the questioning, a few more words on the subject might be relevant.

Naipaul is clinically accurate about the logical progression from self-abasement to self-advertisement to selfishness; he is scrupulous in rendering the motives of the little man who must flog his egotism to succeed in a care-little, do-nothing, failure-oriented society. But the cynicism that sharkfins through these novels and several short stories from the same period —a cynicism that dissects motives and notches out character—eventually hacks away at the drive and energy and exuberance and even naiveté that initially make these characters unique; it whittles away at what is commendable about ambition until we are left with the thinnest sliver of an abstraction on power and fame. Novels about little men jockeying for small power may demand so necessary a paradox. Yet it still seems curious that Naipaul, who managed to escape the enclosure of Trinidad, should ultimately withhold empathy from protagonists who are also trying to escape. We are not likely to empathize with characters with whom the author refuses to empathize. Naipaul diminishes the life force of his nominal heroes by silhouetting them against the color and confusion of a world ambiguously suspended between opportunity on the one hand and inaction and inoperability on the other, or by machining them into cogs stripped of individuality, left to mesh as best they can within the clogged workings of Trinidad's social and political structure. The odd thing about Ganesh and Surujpat is that they begin as almost full-blown characters, only to recede until they are refined out of sight.

Odd, yet not inexplicable, considering a young novelist's exploratory vision and his being faced with the technical difficulty of writing about insularity and heterogeneity without becoming parochial and diffuse. In another way this persistent theme of success and failure also imposed limitations on the vision, for Naipaul was forced to mediate values established by a particular society before turning them into fiction. And the values were opaque and solid enough to prevent a novelist from seeing much beyond what his own characters cared or wanted to see. What I have in mind is found toward the very end of *The Suffrage of Elvira*:

> So, Harbans won the election and the insurance company lost a Jaguar. Chittaranjan lost a son-in-law and Dhaniram lost a daughter-in-law. Elvira lost Lorkhoor and Lorkhoor won a reputation. Elvira lost Mr Cuffy. And Preacher lost his deposit. (p. 207)

This kind of cricketeering value judgment might at first appear ingenuous enough to be ludicrous, but in the contexts of the Trinidadian ethos it is as profound and complex a judgment as one could expect. In a society where material advantage is the initial step to obviating failure at all other levels, the profit-loss, debit-credit mentality can conceive of no other divisions than these simplistic ones. The paradox, if not the ruthless pathos of such a society as Naipaul pictures it in *The Mystic Masseur* and *The Suffrage of Elvira*, is that its profiteers and parvenus and politicians begin in dignity and innocence before they are corrupted by pride and necessity. Almost axiomatically success becomes the end of which corruption is the means. Even acknowledging Naipaul's growing disaffection for Trinidad, I think it likely he was not entirely convinced of this damning logic and that he became concerned with the possibilities of the converse: Can one succeed *without* becoming corrupt? Were there other little men in Trinidad who placed different values on their life in society? Could these Hindus of high caste and low means strive for something beyond the threshold of materialism? Could at least one be found whose expense of spirit did not end in a shame of moral waste?

A House for Mr Biswas tries to answer these questions, though readers of the novel will undoubtedly realize that the biggest of them is the last. For the idea of waste dominates the novel and dogs Mr. Biswas from cradle to grave. As he must in a book so panoramic, Naipaul examines the motif without wrenching from it connotations or gratuitously shaping them for mere effect. Like everything else in this book of ceaseless movement, the idea evolves quite naturally out of the frenzy, noise, and misdirection on the island to become a symbolic extension of the Trinidadian Hindu's life, the sum total of all levels of his existence: in fact, the essence of his existence. Familially, waste is tied to the Hindu's absorption in a collective where continual friction, bickering, rivalry dissipate energies he might better direct elsewhere. Physically, it relates to his mania for cleanliness and the purgative functions, ultimately to his coprophobia. Socially, it points to the disintegration of the Hindu community, a subculture in a society generally incongruous and incoherent. Morally and religiously it embodies the Hindu's shocking apathy and passivity, that lack of drive that leads to what one might call an entropic encounter with Fate.

It is through this undisciplined and diverse world

that Mr. Biswas moves, literally and metaphorically confronting waste and trying to free himself from the communal obsession with it. His life can almost be taken as a compendium of experiences that defines the haphazard and tenacious struggle he undergoes to define himself. There is the waste associated with his early years: the superfluous sixth finger at birth; the foolhardy attempt of his father to retrieve a nonexistent drowned body until he drowns himself; the scatological contretemps when he is studying to be a pundit. There are the many false starts made and futile directions taken before his marriage to Shama Tulsi, the early marriage that in itself wastes his youth. There is the cloacal entrapment of his years with the Tulsis, their sapping of his vitality and of their resources on their various estates. There are, after much too brief an interlude as a notorious journalist on *The Sentinel*, years squandered in hack reporting and of visiting the "Deserving Destitutes"—the "mutilated, the defeated, the futile and the insane living in conditions not far removed from his own." There is that grand moment of disillusionment when he repeatedly pulls the lavatory chain on his *Escape* stories which were to make him famous, and the growing morbidity heightened by encounters with old age and death. And finally, even before his own death, which comes almost as a release, there is the accelerated and paralyzing fear that this life of exhaustion will be played out to the grim end without his having realized his desperate dream: a house of his own.

In this book, Naipaul sets out common milestones that crumble almost immediately after they are set in place and through auxillary markers pointing to Mr. Biswas as flogged, duped, thwarted, cheated, maligned, robbed, humiliated, frustrated, disappointed, and frightened, he charts the small odyssey of a life that is continually confronting and surmounting waste and exhaustion. On the face of things, we seem to be watching the progress of a West Indian Candide undergoing the psychological disassembly of a Lemuel Gulliver, or at times the physical one of Nathanael West's Lemuel Pitkin.

I say "seem." Mr. Biswas' indefatigability in the face of feats and defeats comprises the mere picaresque elements of the novel, and these are tenuous until spun into patterns of contradiction. For while at any one moment in the novel we may point to Mr. Biswas as down, or the next moment as up, in the end we are hard pressed to say whether the book has been about his rise and fall or about quite the opposite. There is no clear cut irony, say, as in Howell's *Silas Lapham* (another novel about housing problems!), where material decline generates a moral and ethical elevation. *A House for Mr Biswas* is more dense and textured, being governed by a kind of Heraclitian paradox in which the way up and the way down are in reality one and the same, a doctrine not at all uncongenial to the Hindu mind. Yet in this case the direction is ambiguously dictated by character and destiny alike, and the acceptance of either is eventually countered by the rejection of both.

What complicates the paradox and the workings of Mr. Biswas' mind is Naipaul's artistic reluctance to allow the conventional attitude to be expressed at the expected moment. Rather than cursing fate when under stress, Mr. Biswas seems accepting of it, while at times of relative well being it is destiny, not his character, to which he accords the blame for past and present failures! When he first comes to Port of Spain, one may remember, a country bumpkin, stranger, and down-and-outer, and is waiting for a doctor to treat a chronic stomach ailment, the illness and sickness about the office cause him to reflect:

> His freedom was over, and it had been false. The past could not be ignored; it was never counterfeit; he carried it within himself. If there was a place for him, it was one that had already been hollowed out by time, by everything he had lived through, however imperfect, makeshift and cheating.[2]

And later, after he has worked his way up to become an established, if not entirely happy journalist, when fluid moments of misanthropy are just hardening into potential paranoia, he rationalizes in the following manner:

> It was now that he began to speak to his children of his childhood. He told them of the hut, the men digging in the garden at night; he told them of the oil that was later found on the land. What fortune might have been theirs, if only his father had not died, if only he had stuck to the land like his brothers, if he had not gone to Pagotes, not become a sign-writer, not gone to Hanuman House, not married! If only so many things had not happened! (p. 396)

These are the preexistential revelations of a hapless Everyman who, like most of us, resists admitting that character is destiny when destiny has given him such a bad shake. And were I seriously disposed to channel these alternating currents of Mr. Biswas' thoughts into the main flow of Hindu philosophy, I would suggest they embrace the doctrines of *dharma* and *karma*: the ethical present predicated on the fixed past and leading to the fated future. But of course Mr. Biswas' accessibility to fate is comic, not philosophic. Naipaul means us to see that his hero's actions are di-

2. *A House for Mr Biswas* (London, 1961), p. 285.

rected as much by the melee and *mélange* of the Indian community, represented by the Tulsi sisters and cousins and aunts, and by his imperfect assimilation of aped and bastardized Western values as by any abstract considerations of conduct. A life so collective, uncontemplative, frenetic, patchwork, and capricious would seem to rule out such austere rules of life as Mr. Biswas could practice or Naipaul write about. Indeed Mr. Biswas does not read the *Bhagavadgita* and the *Vedanta* but Marcus Aurelius and Samuel Smiles, the English Horatio Alger. The one provides stoic support and comfort for his repeated immersions—one might figuratively call them drownings, in view of the preponderance of such imagery in the novel—in a society that tends to absorb and assimilate; the other supplies a continuing hope that by mere plugging away he will emerge from it. What Naipaul fosters through these pulls in contrary directions is a paradox even more refined than the others I have mentioned. Can, he asks, a man foundering from exhaustion in a sea of waste be said not to have wasted his life?

I think any interpretation of the novel trying to reconcile tone and theme and character must be based on this rather singular and important question, though it is more easily asked than answered. What prevents a straightforward "Yes" or "No" is a continuing shift in perspective. We are never quite certain—as we seem to be certain so much of the time in *The Mystic Masseur* and *The Suffrage of Elvira*—how far to press Naipaul's evaluation of Mr. Biswas, Mr. Biswas' evaluation of himself, or ours of both. Understanding Naipaul's persistent and unqualified vision of Trinidad as a place without "rules or patterns" and his disquieting view of the anatomy of the Hindu community within it, we should be surprised to find Mr. Biswas attempts to escape anonymity and obscurity ever amounting to very much. Yet his panicky flailing to gain mobility in a society on the downgrade, perhaps one even retrograde, and his plucky assertions to fight free of apathy and fate bespeak a tentative heroism. Yet again, we must ask if any struggle per se—where defeat seems built in, where limited rise in status seems inconsequential placed alongside the physical and mental depletion—is actually worth it?

To answer "No" to the original question would turn *A House for Mr Biswas* into little more than a sympathetic satire on the underdog, beefed up into the big, broad, driving Great West Indian Novel through its panoramic sweep of Trinidad, its realistic detailing (in the manner of the Edwardian and Victorian novel) of three generations of a family, its descriptive furniture, and its host of various and representative characters. Such a book would be considerable, but hardly as significant as it otherwise might be; it would be predictable, since we do expect the little man to be overwhelmed by life. To be a little man is in fact to be something of a natural-born loser in the best of worlds, and in the most chaotic of them his prefigured decline would be fascinating to watch but not terribly interesting to discuss.

Obviously the interest in *A House for Mr Biswas* lies in Naipaul's answering "Yes," however obliquely, and trying to work out the paradox so that Mr. Biswas at least *seems*, in the end, to rise above the disconnected but potent forces always pulling him down. Like the frog in the well who makes two moves backward for every three forward, he eventually surfaces. But in the course of the novel we become less preoccupied with the goal—for the prologue gives us a capsule summary of all that Mr. Biswas has striven for and achieved—than with the slippery ascent, configurations of which create a more complex pattern than the linear womb-to-tomb narration suggests.

The complexity comes in through Naipaul's juxtaposing the totality of Mr. Biswas' life, which falls into a series of small, critical cycles, with Life itself, rolling on and grinding away with the slowness, irresistibility, and indifference of a juggernaut. It is against such erosion and chaos that Mr. Biswas spends thirty-five of his forty-six years in rebellion, and in quest of a fixed symbol that will restore an order that, but for the drowning of his father, which was significantly as much Mr. Biswas' fault as fate's, would never have been disturbed at all. For he would have been a nobody, but a happy nobody in the village where his father and grandfather were raised; knowing no better he would have been content.

We must not—at least in this first chapter, "Pastoral"—read Naipaul's irony about character and destiny too ambiguously, even though the tone is both tragic and comic. The remote village with its generations of continuity and no-change is a kind of Eden, a paradise of order and predictability that Mr. Biswas is never to experience again until he finally buys his house. It is one pole of shelter and protection he must turn his back on as he stumbles through life toward the opposite pole. Exiled from the garden, unhoused, unparadised, an unlucky, loveless, unexceptional, ambitionless Mohun (whose name means, as though other ironies were not sufficient, "beloved") must try to improve his luck, find love, pursue his talents, court ambition. From a world so ordered that he would never have needed to suffer the agony of choice, he is thrust into another where choice becomes illimitable, where the freedom to choose means to experience the chaos of a world with its "power to frighten," and where to make his stand against chaos and fear depends on his restoring an order so totally lost during his youth.

The trouble is that Mr. Biswas is torn between building his life on two schemes of order. One, what I would call the *order of enclosure*, is established at his marriage into the Tulsis: that entrapping, cloying, overwhelming family that threatens to absorb his character and sap his individuality, but which feeds, shelters, protects, cures, and assures the "success" of its passive dependents. The other, the *order of exposure*, is based on Mr. Biswas' yearning to free himself from this easy entrapment, to go into the world outside, despite its insecurity, hardships, despite the near-Kierkegaardian fear and trembling and anxiety that come from too much freedom, too much choice, too little chance of success. There is a great deal of comedy attached to Mr. Biswas' trials with the first and as much pathos to his disasters with the second. But what Naipaul has drawn best is the schism of self in showing the little man's human weakness and indecision in choosing one order, conclusively, over the other. In fact we are not too far off the mark in seeing him as a rebellious child who flaunts parental care and authority to test himself against the world, always knowing he will be taken back should the world prove too hazardous.

Naipaul's tracing of the daily ins and outs of this proliferating, formidable entity known as the Tulsis is one of the masterstrokes of the novel. Conditioned as we are in America to the "togetherness" of the immediate family only, we may find it hard to fathom Mr. Biswas' initial "elation" at joining the Tulsi clan, herded with all its consanguineous, affinal, and collateral relatives under one roof, and under the matriarchal domination of so immovable and impenetrable a force as Mrs. Tulsi. Yet to concede its peculiar magnetism is to see how Naipaul, with such economy of irony, can rationalize Mr. Biswas' being dunned into marriage. "The world was too small, the Tulsi family too large. He felt trapped." This premise (which is later to admit of many conclusions), his civilized embarrassment at the ill-timed love letter to Shama, his poverty and aimlessness in Pagotes, his good Hindu stock and ethics, and the anticipated largesse to come contribute a great deal toward explaining his early attraction and prolonged submission to the absurd order of the Tulsis.

It is tempting to find in Naipaul's dissection of this order the satire he skirts in the comedy of Mr. Biswas' vacillations, weaknesses, and tribulations. But for all its lack of privacy, petty arguments and jealousies, sibling rivalries, breaches of etiquette, protocol, and ritual, the Tulsi family remains—until it, too, inevitably disintegrates through intermarriages, internal greed and corruption, the American influx of the forties, and the university educations of its scions abroad —a bastion of solidity against the batterings of cultural changes.

What strikes the young Mr. Biswas about his "legal and moral" commitment to the Tulsis—"He was married. Nothing now, except death, could change that."—is that however imprisoned, however "lost, unimportant and frightened" he feels in the "press of daughters, sons-in-law, children," life outside the protective cocoon of Hanuman House is still more menacing and chaotic. The sickness and fatigue uncoiled either by his following the prescribed "patterns" of the Tulsi household or (more difficultly) by his avoiding its proscriptions, also prompt the mild rebellions that bring about the Tulsis' setting him up, first as a storekeeper at The Chase, then as a suboverseer in Green Vale. But the order he must impose on his own life, now that he is a father as well as a husband, inspires superior neuroses. After his disastrous tenure at The Chase, "six years . . . so squashed by their own boredom and futility that at the end they could be comprehended in one glance," he welcomes the enclosure of the Tulsis with a kind of joy:

> Though Hanuman House had at first seemed chaotic, it was not long before Mr Biswas had seen that in reality it was ordered. . . .
> . . . The House was a world, more real than The Chase, and less exposed; everything beyond its gates was foreign and unimportant and could be ignored. He needed such a sanctuary. And in time the House became to him what Tara's [his aunt's] had been when he was a boy. (p. 169)

Except, of course, he is no longer a boy. Experiences at The Chase have tested and wounded him and made him vulnerable enough to retreat into the "sanctuary" of Hanuman House. But such a sanctuary, like the idea of permanent happiness, is false. It grows oppressive because he is once again lost in the crowd, a rung on the Tulsi ladder of precedence, an appendage to their order, never able to assert either independence or dignity. To give Mr. Biswas another shot at both, Naipaul thrusts him into the turmoil at Green Vale and into the realization that being trapped and "free" is preferable to being merely trapped; the anguish of freedom exhausts one only slightly more than the anguish of surrender. It is such a freedom that now brings on his encounters with a "fear" built upon many things (death not excluded) but mostly on the knowledge that our dreams about the future can become nightmares when we sense the future is already upon us.

The whole tempo of *A House for Mr Biswas*, the plot, but most notably Mr. Biswas' character turn on the hopeless, grotesque, and violent episodes at Green Vale: the separation from Shama; the increased difficulty of communicating with his son Anand; the strike and threats of the fieldworkers; the brutal killing of his dog Tarzan; the fiasco attached to the building of his first house and its destruction; and his nervous breakdown. Yet Mr. Biswas is bandied about between desperation and anger, panic and apathy, guilt and accidie without ever losing his resilience. To what artistic purpose? What are we to make of a man who is married, has three children and a fourth on the way, who grubs along for a token wage at a job he loathes, who has no prospects for finding anything better, who sees his house lashed by rain and destroyed by lightning (a mini-Deucalion and holocaust in one), who himself becomes a mental and physical wreck, yet who can prime his psyche with enough energy so that he is again galvanized into action?

> He was going out into the world, to test it for its powers to frighten. The past was counterfeit, a series of cheating accidents. Real life, and its especial sweetness, awaited; he was still beginning. (pp. 274–75)

I suppose one might call such a man, at worst, a fool; at best, an optimist; even, moving on to more tragic alternatives, a kind of martyr or Job. However, Naipaul is sufficiently detached to avoid straitjacketing Mr. Biswas either with the many-colored coat or a hairshirt. He places him in none of these categories: not in the role of the fool because it would satirize the struggle in life, making it seem futile, directed toward nothingness; not in the latter three because each presumes actions are ordered on some preexistent belief. Mr. Biswas maintains his resilience almost to the end, because his belief in and response to order are so protean and kinetic. He wants "order" but paradoxically does not know what the order is. He does know he must escape the enclosure of the Tulsis and plunge into "real life." Entrapment and habit can only waste him further; freedom and flux may create him anew.

The perfection of *A House for Mr Biswas* is that Mr. Biswas never experiences either. He quests after "real life"—life as we wish to fulfill it through our fantasies—and ironically Naipaul lets him find it, along with hard and multifaceted truths: that "real life" does not mean getting what you want but often the contrary; that for people of certain temperament and character and personality life is no more real in one place than in another; that, too often, our dreams of what we wish to be are never realized, owing to our own insufficient talent; that those desiring order may be the last to find it; that, though it may not control character, there is such a thing as fate.

These are the reasons that events in the second half of the novel—set in and around Port of Spain—run, through their cycles of luck and ill-luck, departures and arrivals, beginnings and endings, parallel to those in the first half. Naipaul is not imposing a fatalism or inevitability on Mr. Biswas so much as allowing an archetypal congruity (a kind of eternal recurrence) that most lives take on after a certain point. His sense of well-being and freedom at living apart from the Tulsis amidst the hubbub of Port of Spain is once again dispelled by loneliness, sickness, fear. Even becoming a journalist does not make him content for long; he grows obsessed with becoming a writer. His attempts to demonstrate his "literary" skill in hundreds of revealing *Escape* stories all beginning, "At the age of thirty-three, when he was already the father of four children . . .," are abortive. As his father drowned, so his son almost drowns; as his house at Green Vale was destroyed, so his house at Short Hills is burned to the ground. He perseveres in his credulity about people's integrity and is continually bilked and humbled by them. He succeeds, only to feel he has failed; is "revivified," only to lapse into apathy; surges with ambition, only to be plunged into the "void."

What sustains him through these shifts of character and fate, what in fact drives the novel forward for five hundred pages, is his vision of the house. And just as that overarching vision, along with a dozen related ones (the romance of the city, his youth, his brilliant career, etc.), seems finally to be lost, it just as suddenly materializes. He buys the house at Sikkim Street, almost immediately becomes ill, and four years later dies.

No other symbol in the novel approaches the complexity and intensity of this last house of Mr. Biswas, and Naipaul devotes to it only the final, eleven-page chapter of the book. It is of course both a brilliant and profound novelistic tour, drawing the line between those small, unnoticed, objective anticlimaxes of Life and the subjective Climax of Mr. Biswas' life. By changing the indefinite article of the novel's "*A* House" to the definite article of the chapter's title "*The* House," Naipaul crystallizes the ambiguity of the human condition, in which universal aspirations for perfection and completeness must invariably be housed in something concrete and tangible and thereby be imperfect. It was Wilde who remarked that there are only two tragedies in the world: "One is not getting what one wants, and the other is getting it." But for all that epigram's truth, the truth of *A House for Mr Biswas* burrows more deeply, splitting man into the tragicomic creature he is. For it is the eternal Comedy of Life that forces Mr. Biswas into questing after order, and the Tragedy of Life that allows him at last to find an order where questing no longer becomes important.

With the house at Sikkim Street, Mr. Biswas' dreams become reality; the will-o'-the-wisp, alternately glowing and guttering for forty years and three generations of Biswases, ignites with his rash, fearful, yet inspired purchase. All the frustration and anxiety accrued from failures with the other houses seem to disappear in the security of his last. And despite his initial disenchantment with its imperfections, his progressive disappointment that it constantly needs repairs, Mr. Biswas sees the house bridging the gap between expectation and completion, as the grand symbol of his freedom, personal independence, pride and dignity; and sees it too as redeeming all his past trials, perhaps the very past itself:

> Soon it seemed . . . that they had never lived anywhere but in the tall square house in Sikkim Street. From now their lives would be ordered, their memories coherent. The mind, while it is sound, is merciful. And rapidly the memories of Hanuman House, The Chase, Green Vale, Shorthills, the Tulsi house in Port of Spain would become jumbled, blurred; events would be telescoped, many forgotten. Occasionally a nerve of memory would be touched . . . and a fragment of forgotten experience would be dislodged, isolated, puzzling. . . . later, and very slowly, in securer times of different stresses, when the memories had lost the power to hurt, with pain or joy, they would fall into place and give back the past. (pp. 523–24)

Yet if Mr. Biswas sees things in one way, Naipaul sees them in another. While the house, as a metaphor and as a reality, appears to have freed Mr. Biswas from the order of enclosure he sought to escape and the order of exposure he thought to engage, it really has only prepared a snare more insidious than either. This is the order of completion, of ending. In finally ordering the chaos of life and containing it in his house, Mr. Biswas removes himself from the dangerous flux that gives life meaning and vitality. His energy and will seep away when there is nothing left to struggle for. Simply, now that Mr. Biswas has gotten "the" thing he wanted all along, he loses all purpose in life. "Living had always been a preparation, a waiting. And so the years had passed: and now there was nothing to wait for." If, as Naipaul seems to believe, life progresses from beginning to beginning, then the great nihilism, the greater void comes not when life actually ends but when we think it does. Mr. Biswas' surrender to this easy order that brings on apathy, querulousness, dullness, accedia is the true "death of the heart." And in a way that should surprise no one, though Naipaul here seems to slide too slickly into the obvious, he dies of a heart attack.

There is, however, a coda to Mr. Biswas' fateful tussle with these paradoxes of order, and it resonates significantly against a complementary set of paradoxes to be found in *Mr Stone and the Knights Companion*. It is an odd sort of coda because it looms editorially in the last paragraphs of the prologue, long before the reader can apprehend the dimensions of its truth. I quote these paragraphs in full:

> But bigger than them all [i.e., the kitchen safe, the typewriter, the bookcase, the dining table, the glass cabinet, the car] was the house, his house.
>
> How terrible it would have been, at this time, to be without it: to have died among the Tulsis, amid the

squalor of that large, disintegrating and indifferent family; to have left Shama and the children among them, in one room; worse, to have lived without even attempting to lay claim to one's portion of the earth; to have lived and died as one had been born, unnecessary and unaccommodated. (pp. 12–13)

It is only after finishing the novel that we could possibly understand the monumental importance of the house to Mr. Biswas and, further, understand Naipaul's universal implication that each of us quests after some congruent symbol in which to enclose our own particular and private ideas of order. For Mr. Biswas the house is exactly this—the primary and pristine symbol of shelter, belonging, love, and order that kept his life from being totally wasted, "unnecessary and unaccommodated." That last word, of course, has resonances of its own. It is howled by King Lear on the heath, where the only buttress against the inequities, perversities, follies, stupidities, madness, evil, and chaos of the world is a hovel. It is a word that defines the inchoate predicament of man. In triumphing over it, Mr. Biswas rises above the waste and stagnation of Trinidad to a sort of supremacy, and his square, flawed, ugly house rises above meanness to a kind of mythic grandeur.

MR. STONE'S FABLE OF ORDER

So far as Naipaul has achieved in his fiction anything approaching an affirmation of life and its continuity, it is to be found in *A House for Mr Biswas*. Despite the novel's pathos, it is free from any mawkishness, mostly owing to the persistent ground base of comedy from which Naipaul disallows sentimental dissonances. Nothing unduly tender is to be wrung even from the weariness and deadness of Mr. Biswas' last days. For all his physical wasting away, sporadic erosion of optimism, and dissipation of personal ambition —now reposed, by way of conclusive defeat, in the future of his children—Mr. Biswas does muddle through the caprice and terrors of the world to die with an illusion of order and permanence he alone established. In a sense, the novel can be taken as an apotheosis of the little man. And because in later novels Naipaul moves further and further away from declaring anything positive or encouraging about the human condition, it is a rare book.

Certainly there is a pattern throughout its large canvas that sets it apart from Naipaul's only other major novel, *The Mimic Men*, and from the shorter *Mr Stone and the Knights Companion* (the latter generally considered to be transitional, though, as I hope momentarily to show, much less so than most critics seem to think). The pattern I have in mind is best represented by imagining a series of concentric circles, all having to do with those domains of order that have become the territory peculiar to Naipaul's fiction. The outermost circle I would label the social order, the next the political, then familial, then moral, and the last, the inner circle, the personal. Imagine further that a complementary zone of disorder—a kind of antiworld divided from the first—exists on each of the circumferences save the smallest, and that the more universal the sphere of order–disorder is, the more likely it will allow for tensions, confusion, and oppositions to be set in motion. Graphically, the idea might be represented by the following:

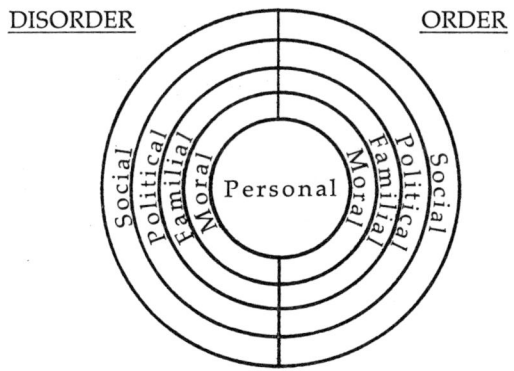

Were I to plot Mr. Biswas' course through the novel, I would say that he begins on the outermost ring, encountering in his centrifugal gyrations exchanges between the various conflicting forces on each level, until just before he dies he reaches the quiet center. The movement in *Mr Stone and the Knights Companion* is centripetal: Its protagonist begins in the innermost circle, entrenched in personal order, and moves outward to reach a newer, if bleaker understanding of a world that all but annihilates his older values.

Both novels, then, are related; they comprise the first and second sections of a four-part structure. Its third section is *The Mimic Men*, where concentric movement in whatever direction has been abandoned to a deviant, polar, eccentric movement beyond the limitations of enclosing spheres. The finale of this piece comes with the novella "In a Free State," where —as we might expect from the title itself—no laws of movement or order seem to operate at all. I of course have no authority for assuming Naipaul's having conceived these novels in this particular way; but their hierarchy of complexity, so far as theme and elaboration are concerned, argues for more than mere tenuous or gratuitous links among them. For if Mr. Biswas pits emotions against fate and manages to escape from nothingness to some sort of order, then Mr. Stone, much less reliant on emotion than on intellect and much more the sport of both fate and character, moves toward recognizing the nothingness of order. Ralph Singh, solely through the assertion of character and the dominance of intellect over emotion, controls fate, yet comes to embrace the order of nothingness; while Bobby becomes the reagent both locked and exiled in a world of reciprocating irrationality. The relationship of the thematic patterning among the novels would look something like this:

Mr. Biswas	Mr. Stone	Mimic Men	Free State
protagonist ruled by emotion	divided between intellect and emotion	controlled by intellect	
and exposed to fate	ambivalent relation to fate and character	ultimate assertion of character	
escape from nothingness to order	recognition of nothingness of order	surrender to order of nothingness	breakdown of perceptions of order and chaos

    I realize this second diagram may seem even a bit more managed than the first. Though since the introduction and, thus far, the critique have throughout stressed Naipaul as a writer who modifies and transforms a basic set of themes from novel to novel and who grows increasingly complex and paradoxical in his modifications, I hope the convenience of the designs will not blemish their substance. What this patterning ultimately suggests to me about the scope of Naipaul's *oeuvre* I would like to reserve for my discussion of *The Mimic Men* and *In a Free State*. Here, I simply wish to use these diagrams as a loose framework for supporting several considerations about the theme and plot of *Mr Stone and the Knights Companion*.

It may seem odd, I grant, to call to mind this latter element about a novel that is at once short and relatively plotless. Yet both qualities in fact sustain, rather than limit, Naipaul's process of directing the reader to the singular expansion of Mr. Stone's consciousness, held throughout these hundred and sixty pages in perfect suspension, and sealed off from multiplying incidents. Only a handful of experiential touchstones are necessary for the protagonist to work out life's final and revealed pattern, though these are gathered in such a way that the casual seems to become the inevitable.

Thus in *Mr Stone and the Knights Companion* the broad strokes of the Caribbean novels are reduced to miniatures; the external world of Trinidad and Port of Spain and the freneticism of Mr. Biswas is translated to English interiors, colorless and conventional London suburbs, and ghastly seasides, and to the automatism of Richard Stone. For psychological reasons (oedipal, but nonetheless murky) Mr. Stone has been socially, sexually, and creatively repressed for sixty-two years. All he can claim to be is what he unprepossessingly is —a librarian, amateur gardener, bachelor—without the hope, or, more pathetically, the thought, of becoming anything more. Habit has choked and clogged him, turned him into something vestigial, a fossil on the banks of time that has never quite entered its stream. Living in this way would make Mr. Stone almost an anachronism in the modern age (the novel is set in the sixties), except he has never really come to grips with the age to begin with. Despite this inertness—or perhaps because of it—he is good, decent, honest, blameless, delighting "more in preparing the ground for planting than in the planting, which sometimes never occurred." Like most who live automatically, Mr. Stone cannot see that his *magister vitae* has produced the *tedium vitae:* Both anticipate some performance that never occurs.

It is important at the beginning of the novel to see Mr. Stone as more taken with preparing than concluding, for there is a final connection to be made between these two processes by the novel's end. Continuous preparation means routine; routine means habit, and habit suggests order that in turn creates the predictability and security that conclusions tend to negate.

> Life was something to be moved through. . . . He was in the habit in odd moments of solitude of writing out neatly tabulated accounts of his career . . . and it always was a marvel to him that the years had gone on, had rolled by so smoothly, that in spite of setbacks and alarms his life had arranged itself with a neatness and order. . . .
> The performance of a habitual action he never rushed . . . And he cultivated his habits. . . .
> . . . There was a tree in the school grounds at the back of his house by which he noted the passing of time, the waxing and waning of the seasons, a tree which daily when shaving he studied, until he had known its every branch. The contemplation of this living object reassured him of the solidity of things. . . . [It was] a re-

minder of the even flowing of time, of his mounting experience, his lengthening past.

All around him were such reminders of solidity, continuity and flow.[1]

Above all else Mr. Stone's solitude fixes the solidity of his life and tallies "neat tabulations" that take everything into account except that life should not perhaps be tabulated. Such mechanical men who march with habit and time can only fear the moment of quickening and revelation that must lead to "upset and disorder." Mr. Stone is not merely a fossil or anachronism; he is an avatar of a dead or atrophying world, an atavism to be found at Prufrockian social teas, at the Misses Morkan's Christmas party in "The Dead," at Clarissa Dalloway's *soirée*. It is, in fact, at an annual Christmas dinner, or shortly afterwards, that Mr. Stone begins to lose his sense of solitude and solidity and to be "overcome by a sense of waste and futility and despair." He suddenly begins to loathe what is solid and permanent because he realizes it will be there when he is gone. Habit, which once supported his resistance to change, now indicates that he, mere flesh, must decay. And so a kind of devilish logic is set in motion with Mr. Stone's first epiphany; to arrest decay he changes habit; he marries.

This is practically all that happens in the opening quarter of the novel, though what does happen is probably more important than I have suggested. Mr. Stone's hermetically sealed world shatters, thrusting him naked of any past attachments into territories of small chaos that he must reorder: no longer, that is, as the benign sexagenarian being eased into retirement

[1]. *Mr Stone and the Knights Companion* (London, 1963), pp. 18–20.

as the little man whose experience and past were "stacked away as neatly" as pudding bowls, one inside the other, but as the disturbed visionary who has "broken the pattern of his life" and through some act of creation now needs to heal the break and/or renew himself.

We are not to question how one as sensitive and intelligent as Mr. Stone has reached the age of sixty-odd without previously experiencing intimations of mortality—those (to quote V. S. Pritchett) "premonitions of Henry Jamesian vastation."[2] The reasons he has not had them are as much a matter of accident and concatenation as the reasons why he at last does. Whether it is owing to the onset of the climacteric, to the loss of solidity, to his sense of existing as a rag-and-bone remnant in a world he doesn't quite understand, to the cold band of fear of death that begins tightening about the heart, or simply to a delayed vision of the self—whether it is because of one or all of these feelings is beside the point. For it is not really a case of "why" he has the insight but "that" he has, since all causality in the novel operates in the present and not, as with *A House for Mr Biswas* and *The Mimic Men*, in a time antecedent to it. On that fatal Christmas Day the premise of "upset and disorder" erases the logic of the past and initiates for Mr. Stone an entirely new argument about life:

> ... he had a realization, too upsetting to be more than momentarily examined, that all that was solid and immutable and enduring about the world, all to which man linked himself ... flattered only to deceive. For all that was not flesh was irrelevant to man, and all that was important was man's own flesh, his weakness and corruptibility. (p. 53)

2. *New Statesman* (31 May 1963), 831–32.

It is from this point on that Naipaul begins playing on the essential paradox attached to Mr. Stone's overhaul of personality and his expanding vision. Gradually he yields to the idea that he must destroy his old self and habits in order to be renewed. And yet all such attempts at renewal and self-generation are found to harbor other elements of destruction. Indeed, as Mr. Stone alternates between contingency and causality, as old habits are replaced by new ones, and as accident opens up entirely new vistas for a creative surge he never knew he possessed, a kind of continuing dialectic between creation and destruction actually takes place. It is man's sense of the "flesh" that beats repeatedly at the brain to corrupt what is even pure and ideal: to corrupt, and again destroy.

Though this revelation does not come until near the end of the novel, Naipaul prepares for it all along the way. I fear, however, that he has not quite decided whether he means to treat literally or symbolically that the destructive force is immanent in the creative urge. In fact I am not certain that one should even consider these presentiments of creation/destruction as literal or symbolic. They haven't the solidity of time and place that one finds supporting the various "houses" in *A House for Mr Biswas*; nor have they the relentless litany of motif one associates with *The Mimic Men*. If anything they are parabolic, shifting from context to context, yet overall they shape a fable of man's being little more than that virgule separating the hospitable order that he imagines he can create from the indifferent or hostile order that actually seems to exist in the universe. How the fable is put together from the experiences of Mr. Stone is a matter of considerable irony as well as art, especially since Naipaul's orderly interlocking of pieces only leads us—as it leads Mr.

Stone—to an acceptance of the irrelevancy of order.

But if Mr. Stone appears at times too much the sport of fate, it is not because the plotting is anywhere aleatory. It instead follows both a diabolical realism and logic: from the first page of the novel (when Mr. Stone's neat, but pathetic flower bed is savaged by a neighbor's cat) to the last (when he is reconciled to a potentially new feline destroyer that has come on the scene). Between these "parentheses"—I borrow Naipaul's own phrase from *The Mimic Men*—ensues the dialectic mentioned above: destruction immanent in creation, endings in beginnings.

Thus in the midst of Christmas week, a London transport poster announcing "muted preparations" for spring lays the groundwork for Mr. Stone's marriage in March to Mrs. Springer—widow, ailurophobe, and coiner of mutual pet names. As "Doggies," the Stones go on holiday to Cornwall to sniff out a dead fox, abandoned Celtic dwellings, and atrophying pensioners. Yet in this "stone-bound land" Mr. Stone becomes unbound and conceives his plan for the Knights Companion, whereby his firm should send out visitors to its pensioned-off employees to make them feel less abandoned and useless, more wanted and in touch. Mr. Stone's chivalrous plan is conceived, I repeat, in the heart of a decaying Cornwall and in a clever and macabre way Naipaul plays off its associations with the coming and passing of Arthur and the Round Table against Mr. Stone's company, which happens to be named Excal. Indeed, as the plan is given *carte blanche* for expansion by the firm's head, Sir Harry, and "licked into shape" by its young, aggressive, and manic PRO man, Whymper, the unconscionable punning on allusions to Arthurian legend endows the idea with a fabled grandeur out of all proportion to its practical, or even ideal genesis. The simple and ingenuous inspiration to rescue men from "inactivity," protect them from "cruelty," keep alive in them "loyalty to the company" swells into a promotional bubble beyond either Whymper or Mr. Stone's imagination and carries both of them to the heights of "success."

And yet Mr. Stone's "success"—the first, and probably only one of his life—produces in him feelings of deflation and failure unparalleled by anything previously experienced. For he is nudged into the dreadful knowledge that his plan has succeeded not because of the beauty of its simplicity and the purity of its conception, but because it has been complicated and corrupted in its realization. Whymper's energetic appropriation of the scheme as his own ("He said he made nothing. 'But,' he added, 'I make something out of nothing.' "), its mutilation in the toils of the packaging machine (devised for the "protection of the old" it is progressively manipulated to "spread the fame of Excal"), and even its inevitable abuse by the recruited Knights Companion representatives do not ruin it in the eyes of Sir Harry, the corporate world, the press, nor the pensioners themselves, but on the contrary assure its success. Although under these circumstances the success of the plan might seem ironic as the world and publicity men and consumers wag, there is very little ironic about it at all. The ironies attach solely to Mr. Stone, whom Naipaul exposes to a second series of "upsets and disorders" more devastating than the first:

> Out of his life had come this one idea; for this single creation his life had been changed for good, perhaps destroyed. And it had gone to magnify Whymper, young Whymper, whose boast was that he made nothing. . . .

> ... Other people had made his idea their property, and they were riding on his back. They had taken the one idea of an old man, ignoring the pain out of which it was born, and now he was no longer necessary to them. Even if he were to die, the Whympers and Sir Harrys would continue to present *Excali*burs. He would be forgotten together with his pain: a little note in the house magazine, then nothing more....
>
> ... So at last the brilliance dimmed, and all that remained was this anxiety, anger and sense of loss. (pp. 108, 125–26)

That Mr. Stone now finds himself in the position of the pensioners he has salvaged is a play on pathos and irony both. But Naipaul is doing more than reviving our stereotypic response to the neglect of old age or capitalizing on the easy cliché of *sic transit*. Mr. Stone's second crucial revelation is undoubtedly pertinent, and one of the novel's peripheral themes; age does feel life's coming and passing more keenly than youth, and in a way that might conceivably be called tragic. Yet there is something here that goes beyond emotional contexts, beyond tracing a succession of optimistic beginnings (marriage with Mrs. Springer, the Knights Companion inspiration, its success and Mr. Stone's success along with it) into pessimistic endings, beyond even capturing very meaningful glimpses into the vanity of accomplishment and previews into obscurity. There is (if we are still convinced of the novel's allegorical or fabulistic nature) beyond it all a glum but germane metaphysics: that any artistic creation must finally become for the artist a "failure," insofar as art makes infinite demands on what is finite, and being but one more artifact of man must itself be reckoned as finite.

Mr. Stone does not syllogize in quite this way, but

what he does think toward the end of the novel means much the same thing:

> Nothing that came out of the heart, nothing that was pure ought to be exposed. . . .
> . . . the only true moments were those he had spent in the study, writing out of a feeling whose depth he realized only as he wrote. What he had written was a faint and artificial rendering of that emotion, and the scheme as [practiced] was but a shadow of that shadow. . . . All action, all creation was a betrayal of feeling and truth. And in the process of this betrayal his world had come tumbling about him. There remained to him nothing to which he could anchor himself. (p. 149)

Mr. Stone is not the first to discern the spirit of nihilism latent in the killing letter of Platonism, though it is certainly curious to find an imaginative and prolific writer like Naipaul promoting such a vision by way of analogy with the creative imagination. Rarely does a Naipaul paradox echo falsely, but here, where we are expected to evolve something universal from a fussy personal disillusionment, I think it does. Art, because it will continue to exist long after us, must always heighten our sense of transitoriness; yet it is this very art, this very act of continuous and creative ordering, that makes us aware of life—its "feeling and truth"—to begin with. This is partially what Rilke meant when he wrote about the "most visible joy" only revealing itself to us after we've "transformed it within," and what Yeats meant when he acknowledged that man's curse and condition was to be in love with what vanishes. I should hope in this case that Naipaul does not share his protagonist's feelings, for once we cease creating—or simply cease becoming—we must surrender to nihilism: the ultimate, undefining, uncreative act.

Yet on this count Naipaul has made Mr. Stone's feelings most convincing. With his revelation of betrayal all "anger, anxiety and sense of loss" mount. The notion that he was before betrayed by what was solid and permanent in the mundane order of things is now enhanced by seeing the purer creative order humbugged as well, and he is left, inevitably and despairingly, with a sense of impermanence and disorder. Looking into his heart to write, he has emptied it of all he ever had to give and finds both heart and creation hollow. At this point a lesser novelist would have obviously seen to it that a copy of *L'Être et le Néant* somehow found its way into his protagonist's hands. But the novel succeeds precisely because Naipaul resists the obvious: resists reducing what Mr. Stone believes is the essential self to the existential one. For whether Mr. Stone's "truth" about life—his recognition of the nothingness of order—remains everyone's truth, Naipaul leaves hanging in a delicate balance.

The counterweight is young Whymper, who, in his bravado, vitality, cynicism, and frantic sexuality emerges not only as Mr. Stone's arch-foil in the novel, but as the prototype of simon-pure materialism in the world. The Whympers who go through life using others, riding on the coattails of the more inspired, charming and seducing (in this case Mr. Stone's homely niece, Gwen), moving on to bigger and better jobs by making "something out of nothing" are perhaps the most secure and unviolated. Naipaul's melancholy suggestion is that the Bishop-of-Bray Whympers, responding to any order, will eventually inherit the earth that has become correlative with their great, destroying will:

> The order of the universe, to which he had sought to ally himself [thinks Mr. Stone on the novel's final pages]

was not his order. So much he had seen before. But now he saw, too, that it was not by creation that man demonstrated his power and defied this hostile order, but by destruction. By damming the river, by destroying the mountain, by so scarring the face of the earth that Nature's attempt to reassert herself became a mockery. (pp. 158-59)

Because the birth and death of Mr. Stone's idea is wrapped up with the imminence of old age and the transitoriness of art, Naipaul's concluding paradox on man's "works and days" has considerable force, but it has a vulnerability as well. For in the end it *is* only an idea that has been violated, and that from without. After having glimpsed eternity and an order not his, Mr. Stone can nevertheless, a "destroyer" though undestroyed, retreat to his study and anticipate the time "when calm would come again." He has, with some pain and difficulty, "survived." How much more qualitatively difficult and painful survival becomes Naipaul takes up in his next novel: almost, it would seem, by entering Ralph Singh's seedy bed-sitting room through the back door of Mr. Stone's cheery study. That novel is *The Mimic Men,* and one of its themes is violation not from without but from within, and in it, not merely an idea or scheme becomes a "shadow of a shadow," but a man.

THE MIMIC MEN: "ORDER, SEQUENCE, REGULARITY"

*T*HE *Mimic Men*—Naipaul's masterpiece to date—did not follow hard on the heels of *Mr Stone and the Knights Companion.* The gap of four years was significant, and fortunate. For after his critical success with *Mr Stone,* Naipaul was faced with the problem of what sort of novel to write. He could continue writing about England as an outsider turned insider, about Trinidad as an insider now become outsider, or he must find something new entirely. Two of these alternatives were perhaps more theoretical than viable.

Take (strictly on conjecture) the first: another "English novel." In retrospect I see the choice not only as limiting but possibly as redundant. However perfectly wrought and polished an intaglio, *Mr Stone and the Knights Companion* has neither the depth, scope, warmth, nor humanity of *A House for Mr Biswas.* Understandably so. Although Naipaul was writing about certain concepts with which he seemed intimate enough, he was conveying them through characters and settings that had only recently become familiar to him. As an expatriate, Naipaul did offer fresh insights about the English scene and on the English little man, but Mr. Stone's character was subordinated in some sense to the larger issues of the novel; and even these larger issues were almost residual compared to the one great, volatile theme that had potential significance beyond a single man, beyond English urban or suburban life, beyond England itself. What was Naipaul to make further of Mr. Stone's belated vision of human power lodged in human weakness, of this recognition of a solipsism so perfect that the ego could define itself at the expense of creation *or* destruction? And what vehicle could support the paradoxes generated by these dual, man-made orders?

The second choice also seemed unlikely. Naipaul still knew Trinidad best, but he had played out the main themes of Trinidadian success and failure in Mr.

Biswas' drama. The book had been acclaimed by most (British) reviewers as the definitive Caribbean novel, and it would not make much sense for Naipaul to try for the same effect a second time and possibly fail. Again, despite its panoramic sweep, despite the mythic suggestiveness of its widening circles, *A House for Mr Biswas* centers the protagonist's quest for order within an exclusive Hindu cultural pocket stitched round by even narrower perimeters than those bordering the exurbia of *Mr Stone and the Knights Companion*. Naipaul had surely written the epic of a colonial, but was it quite the same thing as a colonial epic?

There is probably enough here to suggest why Naipaul chose neither mode for his next novel and why *A House for Mr Biswas* and *Mr Stone and the Knights Companion* both directly influenced *The Mimic Men*. In perfect outline, but with many of the details to be fleshed out, the unresolved themes of the lesser Caribbean books that found their way into *A House for Mr Biswas* anticipate those in *The Mimic Men*. Ganesh, Surujpat, and Mohun Biswas are, in fact, Naipaul's first "mimic men," still lacking the force of history to thrust them into tragic significance. And almost independently of what it has to say, *Mr Stone and the Knights Companion* can be seen as an advance on Naipaul's complex responses to an England—and a London—that later reasserts itself as the framework outside the "parentheses" of the Caribbean drama enclosing *The Mimic Men*. Once we are aware that Naipaul's responses to his English as well as to his Caribbean material are primarily cultural, we can see that all the books up to *The Mimic Men* reflect a deepening understanding of his alienation from the two cultures that shaped him and, no less importantly, from a third culture. It was Naipaul's thorough rejection of his Indian heritage that turned him into something of a permanent *deraciné* and matured the vision of the triple exile that reaches dimensions of tragedy in *The Mimic Men*. Without first having written *An Area of Darkness,* Naipaul could not have written the great colonial epic that he at last did write.

An Area of Darkness is the vivid and penetrating account of Naipaul's *Wanderjahre* in India. The experience was both illuminating and shattering. India stirred atavistic memories, lured Naipaul into almost believing he belonged there. But in the end, his quest for the roots that his grandfather had transplanted in Trinidad and that had nourished his (Naipaul's) own conflicting attitudes and allegiances as an inheritor of three cultures confirmed more deeply still his intimations of being a permanent exile. Modern India appeared to Naipaul even more a culturo-colonial paradox than the modern West Indies:

> The outer and inner worlds do not have the physical separateness which they had for us in Trinidad. They coexist; the society only pretends to be colonial; and for this reason its absurdities are at once apparent. Its mimicry is both less and more than a colonial mimicry. It is the special mimicry of an old country which has been without a native aristocracy for a thousand years and has learned to make room for outsiders, but only at the top. The mimicry changes, the inner world remains constant: this is the secret of survival.... Yesterday the mimicry was Mogul; tomorrow it might be Russian or American; today it is English.
>
> Mimicry might be too harsh a word for what appears so comprehensive and profound.... But mimicry must be used... because so much of what is seen remains simple mimicry, incongruous and absurd; and because no people, by their varied physical endowments, are as capable of mimicry as the Indians.[1]

1. *An Area of Darkness* (Baltimore, 1968), pp. 56–57.

So much for the outward show, the façade, the "casual confidence trick" (as he puts it elsewhere) the English had played on the entire society. A more indelible impression was made after Naipaul's return to London, when he recollected in tranquility ("facing [his] own emptiness, [his] feeling of being physically lost") how such a world of mimicry and shadows was merely absorbed into a Hindu world of illusion, and how that world might easily and insidiously absorb anyone who at last grew tired of the game:

> We talk of despair, but true despair lies too deep for formulation. It was only now, as my experience of India defined itself more properly against my own homelessness, that I saw how close in the past year I had been to the total Indian negation, how much it had become the basis of thought and feeling. And already, with this awareness, in a world where illusion could only be a concept and not something felt in the bones, it was slipping away from me. I felt it as something true which I could never adequately express and never seize again. (pp. 266–67)

This is, however, precisely what Naipaul did seize upon and express three years later, and I believe I understand why. The corollary to his having confronted a complex of devastating attitudes, having been tempted to succumb to them, having mastered the impulse to do so, and having written a book about the experience was that he would write yet another book showing how different the design might have been had he yielded to the temptation. *The Mimic Men* seems to me this sort of book. Autobiography becomes fiction; the "area of darkness" that was India becomes, through a shift in the spirit of time and place, a composite of Trinidad and England; the mimicry of the Anglo-Indian becomes that of the British-educated Hindu colonial; and "negation" becomes the analogue for the game of illusion that has been the life of the refugee–immigrant, narrator–hero. R. R. K. Kripalsingh (Ralph Singh), who, at forty, having exhausted his role as friend, countryman, lover, as son and husband, as student, businessman, politician, diplomat, now writes his life from an "unchanging room" in a middle-class London hotel and strives to secure in the "inaction" imposed upon him "the final emptiness."

Singh's London room provides the literal framework for *The Mimic Men*, but at the end of the novel it becomes apparent that it has all the while been a basis for the symbolic structuring as well. I say "room"; more exactly it is two rooms, though each is congruent with the other, the two sides of the same worn and spent coin that is Singh's life. The first such is the attic room in the boardinghouse in Kensington where he takes up temporary residence after the war and begins his "preparation for life": his initial taste of unlimited freedom outside the dusty village on "Isabella" (Trinidad): his entanglements with the great and chaotic city of London; his strange, questing career as student and voluptuary; his marriage to the white girl, Sandra. The second room, that in the hotel, he inhabits fifteen years later. Now in exile and obscurity, ravaged and drained by the flux of history, defeated by personal, social, political, and cultural forces, fragmented, he seeks to understand and ratify through the writing of his life the final "withdrawal" from it.

Rooms are the alpha and omega of Singh's existence, and Naipaul extends the range of his symbol by working the paradoxes inhering in it. In a novel dealing with displacement and loneliness, with desolation, dissolution, with failed ambitions, the last room becomes a mausoleum of claustrophobia and deadness. It images the no-exit of Sartrean confinement, the paralysis of Beckettian silence and inaction. At the same time it is a Proustian room in which Singh tries to reconstruct from memory—memory being but another mimic action of reality—the "parentheses" of a life enclosed by the only two fixed points he has ever known: the twin ports between which he has experienced the "shipwreck" that is his life. Logically, the two rooms would seem to mark this beginning and end, the "preparation" and "withdrawal." Metaphysically, though, they are continuous, the last a consequence of the first.

For while an inhabitant of the first, Singh, the imperfectly Westernized Hindu, becomes dominated by the driving illusion of Western man, lodged (as Lévi-Strauss tells us in *The Savage Mind*) in the psychological materialism of Freud and the historical materialism of Marx—the idea of a goal:

> The living material of Freud [one of Lévi-Strauss's brilliant commentators goes on to say] aspires to the nirvana of inert matter; it wants to come to rest at unity but it is doomed to move and divide, to desire and hate the forms it engenders. The historical man of Hegel and Marx wants to suppress his otherness, to be one again with others and with nature, but he is doomed to change himself constantly and to change the world.[2]

It is this belief in a goal—most immediately embodied in the libidinous, protean, "whitey-pokey" Sandra—that Singh takes back with him to Isabella; this belief that initiates his drive toward wealth and power; this belief (in the end mere illusion) that amplifies the discord between what he is and what he thinks he is.

Thus the last room offers the devestating reduction of the illusion, the true annihilation of substance for Singh. He sees that what he believed to be the sub-

2. Octavio Paz, *Claude Lévi-Strauss: An Introduction* (Ithaca, 1970), p. 125.

stantive part of his life was mere shadow, mere mimicry; he writes his history, hoping in part to abolish it, as though it is only through disintegration that he can assess its meaning. In part, too, the writing itself becomes a process of life that reconciles Singh to his lost heritage. Like his father, Gurudeva, who leaves his family to become a holy mendicant, a *sunyasi*, Singh, a waiter, no longer need regard change as a manifestation of energy (a strictly Western prejudice), but Brahmin-like as the illusory realm of impermanence. The irony of allowing a Hindu, whose philosophy teaches the negation of history, to withdraw from life in order to write history is one of the finest in the novel. But to fully value it I think we must understand that Singh's life ultimately shows how the world of varied, chance events leads to a limbo where being and nothingness are absorbed. In the end, we find a man tricked by what he imagined was permanent power and the illusion of freedom, by the chimera of a goal; now he can but contemplate "an apparatus which knows no activity other than repetition, and which lacks a goal." The process produces one of Naipaul's subtlest divinations of order. Singh's unconscious has almost *consciously* gained "the knowledge of the void."

There is yet a more unifying irony that should return us to my conviction that this last room is the novel's symbolic center and will provide something of a springboard for my discussing *The Mimic Men* in terms of its themes and overall structure. By way of setting things in motion, let me quote the crux of the brief, but significant passage from which I have already taken bits and snippets. It is to be found half a dozen or so pages from the end of the novel:

> It never occurred to me that the writing of this book might have become an end in itself, that the recording

of a life might become an extension of that life. It
never occurred to me that I would have grown to relish
the constriction and order of hotel life, which previously
had driven me to despair; and that the contrast between
my unchanging room and the slow progression of what
was being created there would have given me such
satisfaction. Order, sequence, regularity: it is there
every time the electric meter clicks, accepting one more
of my shillings. (p. 293)

"Order, sequence, regularity!" This quintessence
of "pattern" for which Singh has all along quested,
hoping to understand how seemingly random events
and accident have created the fractured self is revealed
in the emptiness of an exile's room. The revealed pattern is, however, only a shadow of the real pattern he
has lost. And the revelation comes, as such revelations
usually do, without éclat. Singh's beast does not spring
from the jungle of tangled relationships, fraudulent
motives, conditional acts. It circles him, continually,
elusively. He is ontogenically drawn, rather than suddenly galvanized, into knowing why "[his] own journey, scarcely begun, had ended in the shipwreck which
all [his] life [he] had sought to avoid." And in pondering why, in his freedom to choose, he made at every
turn the wrong choice; why he continued to enforce
the imagined projection of himself and fill the void
with the mere mimicry of coherence, he unveils by degrees how the quest for order dissolved into chaos,
how sequence surrendered to contingency, how regularity whirled off into eccentricity.

These are, I think, the principal movements in
The Mimic Men that articulate many of its themes and
its structure. And since the second of these movements
is tied in with the novel's outline, I should like to discuss it first.

Singh's reconstruction of the past is, one may

remember, more than autobiographical. His life is very much interwoven with the political and social changes taking place on Isabella and consequently aspires to being pseudo- or quasi-history as well. Yet the idea of any sequence common to the writing of history is slyly undermined by Naipaul's method of narrative: a discriminating selection of facts by memory, rather than an impartial, logical presentation of them. What I mean to suggest here is that the novel's architectonics are at odds with the idea of historic continuity, with the pattern that Singh would like but is unable to realize.

To be more specific, the novel covers more than a quarter of a century, from about 1930 when Singh is ten until 1960 when he is forty; it opens on a date midway between, 1946, and moves backward before moving forward. A modern reader has no trouble accepting this convention as a respectable mode of memory–narrative, but Naipaul works a curious and pertinent variation on the technique. Singh's memory seems to blur as the novel moves closer to the present. Facts become opaque; hiati appear between large chunks of time unaccounted for. Events become shadowy contingencies as Singh himself withdraws further and further into the private world that casts him into shadowy relief, until, by the end of the novel, he is no more than a face peering out from behind a pillar.

It is the second and longest section of the novel, dealing with Singh's childhood, adolescence, and initiation into manhood, that is the most vivid. Isabella, not yet a dream but still very much a reality, is fixed in time and space and given historic solidity in that James Anthony Froude had once visited there and written about it. For Singh, son of a poor schoolteacher, though allied on his mother's side to the millionaire owners of the Bella Bella Coca-Cola Bottling Plant, the island is a place of paradox and tensions. He is fascinated by wealth and poverty alike; he is drawn to his rich cousin Cecil and to the less rich, but more aristocratic Creole family of the Deschampsneufs; yet he is also attracted to the struggling, ambitious blacks like Hok and Browne. Like them he loathes the daily "betrayals into ordinariness," cherishes their secret dreams of escape from Isabella, and dreams himself, inflamed by his reading in *The Aryan Peoples and Their Migrations*, of fulfilling the prophecy incarnate in his surname ("Singh," "one of the warrior caste") by ruling the island.

Up to a certain point in this section, Naipaul appears to be reworking the themes of escape and betrayal found in his earlier Caribbean books, with the exception that something complete seems struggling to be born out of Singh's half-formed ego. But whatever it is fails to materialize. Chance thwarts will; his search for continuity, his desire to participate in life become detoured through chance events that confirm how much more easily and more naturally man destroys than creates. The illumination of Mr. Stone still burns with a frightening incandescence.

The lesson is brought home to Singh in a dozen ways, and at each turn he is maimed anew. His uncle's shame and savage desire for revenge after the near collision of his truck with some workers imbue him with intimations of power; his father's desertion and subsequent affiliation with radical insurgents shatter his foundations of family and stability; the drownings at the beach and the gross attitudes of the fishermen desensitize him to pity, make him retrench further into the role of observer in order to avoid further wounding; the evisceration of the Deschampsneufs' prize racehorse (by his father's followers and according to the ancient Indian blood rite of *Asvamedha*) renders obscene his long love affair with Aryan myth; and his near-shooting of his half-brother during their macabre beach ramble almost pushes him to becoming a participant in destruction rather than simply an observer of it.

I hope the substance of the above (and following) catalogue will excuse, somewhat, their utilitarian rhetoric, for to understand these lacerations of the child and young man is to understand partially the insulation and masochism of the adult. Singh's responses to events in England after the war—his womanizing with pick-ups and prostitutes, the disturbing and febrile courtship of Sandra, marriage to her—and those covering a decade on Isabella before his final exile—his shabby dealings and calculated successes in real estate, Sandra's divorce and departure, his period of solitude in the "Roman" house, the founding with Browne of *The Socialist*, his rise to power as head of the country and his ouster—are all conditioned by the maimings in youth.

Yet, placed cheek by jowl, the events are unshaped by meaning or consequence. They are disjointed appendixes affixed to a text of total negation. The more powerful Singh becomes publicly, the more isolated he grows personally; the more he exercises control over others, the less he can stave off the encroaching impotence of mind and body; the more in touch with the masses he seems, the less able he is to reenter the mainstream of humanity. *Je vens d'lué*, he says at the end of the novel, using the patois of Isabella. *From* where, we know. But *to* where? Singh has so admirably realized his youthful avowal to "eliminate" all superfluous things from life, to "simplify," that he has pushed elimination and simplification to the near vanishing point, and with it all feeling, contact, desire, development. Annihilated by the forces of contingency he has permitted to control it, the sequence of his life is now merely a matter of record: as accurate, unvaried, embalmed as the striations on his desk and the patterned wallpaper in his "unchanging room."

Singh's quest for "sequence," or the historic order of *The Mimic Men*, is synchronous with the search for "regularity," or personal order. In one way this particular movement hangs together through Naipaul's use of motif: here a symbol, there a phrase, but in either case peculiar to the patterns eluding Singh throughout. Motif is not baffling in *The Mimic Men*. On the contrary, it is rather transparent, for much of the novel's paradox is lodged in Singh's refining to obscurity what could have been so patently obvious. One will readily see, for example, that reiterations of the "two landscapes of sea and snow" (Isabella and England) between which Singh is restlessly driven, correspond to his private shipwreck and the crystalline perfection of his desolation; or that the periods of his life are linked to the women he has known—his mother, Lieni, Sandra, Wendy, Stella, indeed even Isabella—and betrayed, or with whom infatuation has fallen into ennui, disgust, impotence. A phrase returns to mirror his *Sehnsucht* (*"Who comes here? A grenadier. What does he want? A pot of beer."*), another to echo the cry of the defeated in the war between master and slave ("The Niger is a tributary of that Seine") and to inspire his first paper of political theorizing; still another (*"Quantum mutatus ab illo"*) to invoke the discontinuity he experiences through change and loss.

There are not many motifs, and I repeat, they are

not difficult to trace. Nor are they intended to further involute the difficulties inherent in Naipaul's demanding narrative. He uses them, like James and Proust, to force breathing spaces between the closely woven textures of prose (and do double service in a novel containing only several dozen lines of dialogue), to bridge (or merge) the past and the present, and to sustain the exchanges between time and memory. He uses them like Woolf and Joyce to give his protagonist a kind of moment-to-moment solidity amidst the flux of word and world. And he uses them in a witty and relevant way that is singularly his own, as a technique underlining the novel's central theme of mimicry. For it is repetition and simulation that haunt Singh from childhood onward: quite consciously at first, but then so mechanically as to have become a kind of biological art.

In his initial impersonation—when a boy of about ten—he "suppresses the connection" with his father's family, for "to be descended from generations of idlers and failures, an unbroken line of the unimaginative, unenterprising and oppressed, had always seemed . . . to be a cause for deep, silent shame." He temporarily shuffles off the shame by signing his compositions "Ralph Singh" (his real name being Ranjit Kripalsingh) but a piece of him gets lost in that shuffle and in subsequent ones. A witness to his uncle's fiasco with the lorry driver, he learns that "a man was only what he saw of himself in others"; at school he falls easily into the role of "natural impersonator"; and a dangerously unsporting attitude is struck on the cricket field:

> An audience is never important. An audience is made up of individuals most of whom are likely to be your inferiors. . . . The successful public performer in whatever field operates, not perhaps from contempt, but from a profound lack of regard for his audience. The

actor is separate from those who applaud him; the leader, and particularly the popular leader, is separate from the led. (p. 136)

Yet though Singh grows more calculating in developing those nascent powers of mimicry that finally generate the mimicry of power, he cannot escape the atavistic taint: the proclivity, owing to some unaccountable combination of forces, to be enslaved by his own expertise, cast by it into an existential limbo:

> We, here on our island, handling books printed in this world, and using its goods, had been abandoned and forgotten. We pretended to be real, to be learning, to be preparing ourselves for life, we mimic men of the New World, one unknown corner of it, with all its reminders of the corruption that came so quickly to the new. (p. 175)

This, perhaps the most lucid perception in the novel, is never surpassed. It becomes both justification and rationalization for Singh's strange *decision*—I underscore the word to make it perfectly clear that he has not yet relinquished the illusion of freedom—to purge the inward "corruption" by spreading it endemically. Devious and eccentric acts raise the supreme barrier, in front of which he can mime public gestures, behind which he can retreat into a private fantasy of coherence. Against tradition he marries a "whitey-pokey," thereby cutting himself off from Isabella's "society"; he plays the arch-capitalist by engineering a condominium development called, in honor of his father, Kripalville, and sees the name transformed by popular wits into a symbol of his own maiming, Crippleville. He entombs himself in the opulent, grotesque Roman house, setting the stage for his rise from patrician to politician; and even when he and Browne create the "movement" on Isabella (or rather as he conjectures, when the "movement" creates them), there is fraudulence latent in his idealism. For he capitalizes on the rumored intimacy between himself and Wendy Deschampsneufs, becoming, "at least in so far as appearances went, what others saw in me. It was play for me, play for her."

Except the play eventually becomes life, or indistinguishable from it. Every act, every gesture, every plan and detail are effected by Singh with an eye to the drama; game playing is no longer the means to an end but the end in itself, since it brings with it its own rules, its own sense and idea of personal order:

> So we brought drama of a sort to the island [Singh writes after his party has come to power]. I will claim this as one of our achievements. Drama, however much we fear it, sharpens our perceptions of the world, gives us some sense of ourselves, makes us actors, gives point and sometimes glory to each day. . . .
> . . . Drama buoyed me up in my activity. . . . Now we, the chief actors, however powerless, however finally futile, were public figures, remarked on wherever we went. There was drama in that power game, from which I had withdrawn. . . . Drama walked with us . . . I will claim it as an achievement, though the consequences for me were far from pleasant. (pp. 256–57)

That ironic coda (tacked on by way of a subordinate, and litotes to boot) does more here than wag the dog. The game and the drama account for Singh's success; they also engineer his failure. For under this sort of *modus operandi*—is it not the normal mode of all corrupt governments?—one miscalculation or miscue unmasks the rules governing the arbitrary regularities of play as the false classifications they are. What Singh discovers too late is that the master of a role is always only an ace away from becoming its prisoner. Singh falls from power in the literal and figurative senses with all substance (moral and material) dissipated. And having given over, at forty, the complexities demanded by life, he can only drift away from "responsibility and attachment" toward the "final emptiness," retreat into shadowy simplicity, and—the paradox is Naipaul's, not mine—become a slave to the total and useless freedom he has so long courted.

In the end, such freedom negates all will, all desire to be anything but free. There is a more terrifying paradox reserved for Singh, a more unique tragedy for the "warrior" who is left with the "fear of action," for the virile politico who is reduced to sterility and impotence. As Lawrence wrote more than fifty years ago in *Women in Love*, this sort of freedom is "the substitution of the mechanical principle for the organic, the destruction of the organic purpose, the organic unity, and the subordination of every organic unit to the great mechanical organization. This is the first and finest state of chaos." Singh's resolution of all conflict that forces his life into mechanical order is the sag into chaos. And it is this idea Naipaul uses as the organizing metaphysics of the novel, beyond which even Singh's quest for historic and personal order pales: his making ultimately tangible the chaos from within.

The dense layers and fine textures of *The Mimic Men* and its leaps back and forth in time make it difficult to assess the exact moment that the movement from "playacting to disorder" (the words are Singh's) realizes the final pattern. Nor perhaps would this kind of assessment be of particular value. Naipaul's metaphysics are generated along antithetical, rather than syllogistic lines. Every one of Singh's actions is matched by a counteraction. Marriage ends in divorce, riches in poverty, success in failure, power in helplessness, respect in scorn, popularity in isolation, creation in destruction. In a dozen ways Singh's immersion in life and history brings about exile from them; he begins with "the human instinct for order" and steers voluntarily toward "shipwreck." Certainly this, the most salient motif and metaphor in *The Mimic Men*, catches perfectly the whole, dreary, conscious drive toward "controlled chaos."

Still, in a novel emphasizing that drive toward a goal that is goallessness, Naipaul does make an assessment of sorts. He compresses ideas adumbrated in the Caribbean books and *Mr Stone and the Knights Companion* into several major statements on chaos and order—especially as they pertain to politics and power—and works all four themes together wherever they suit the novel's design. It is not fortuitous, that is, that Singh first collides with intimations of metaphysical order after the near collision on the dusty road in Isabella; it is not fortuitous either that he dreams at this moment (when the political and dramatic are yoked violently together) of becoming head of the country; and it is not fortuitous that when he does become topdog on Isabella these particular ideas of order suddenly evanesce. Although in Naipaul's perspective the occurrences are not fortuitous, for Singh they could well be. In the one case, that of the boy and his uncle and a lorry driver on a road, Singh resurrects a vision of order from potential chaos. In the other, that of the vulnerable politician in the "Roman" house (more an ironic device than an architectural structure, since inspiration for its design came from similar houses at Herculaneum and Pompeii), chaos has devolved from the height of order. It is hard under such circumstances not to accept paradoxes of existence whereby chaos and order, almost interchangeable, lead to an identical nullity:

> My career is by no means unusual [writes confessional Singh retrospectively at the opening of the novel]. It falls into the pattern. The career of the colonial politician is short and ends brutally. We lack order. Above all, we lack power, and we do not understand that we lack power. We mistake words and the acclamation of words for power; as soon as our bluff is called we are lost. Politics for us are a do-or-die, once-for-all charge. Once we are committed we fight more than political battles; we often fight quite literally for our lives. . . . For those who lose, and nearly everyone in the end loses, there is only one course: flight. Flight to the great disorder, the final emptiness. . . . (pp. 10–11)

Though in the way of all "colonial" novels *The Mimic Men* is political as well, thematically bound up with the nature of power, Naipaul has tried to extend this almost ungraspable concept beyond aphorism and vague and unreliable generic definitions. For Singh—the participant in an ambiguous drama, a man who does not possess the "frenzy, the sense of mission, the necessary hurt" required for the professional politician—power goes beyond the impudent, the corrupting, the mechanical, the dehumanizing. It is something more than a historic adjunct to the Hobbesian contract emerging from the chaos of meanness, shortness, brutality, nastiness. Power is a dialectical phenomenon, but it is also a manifestation of chance and revelation. It is a frightening noumenon of time and place. It is a destroyer of substance, a creator of shadow men. It is a self-generating entity feeding upon itself only to devour itself and all aligned with it. "The tragedy of power like mine," writes Singh, "is that there is no way down; there is only extinction."

Merely to encounter this rather overwhelming metaphysic—power as leading to "extinction," nothingness, the void, emptiness—is perhaps to glimpse *why* power can create the most destructive delusions in those whom chance calls upon to wield it. However much we may mistrust and abhor power, we have come to regard it as one of the few inescapable constructs of our civilization, from Alexander on: indeed, the single force that has made our civilization—for good or ill—what it is. Yet if we follow Naipaul's line in *The Mimic Men*, we are beset by certain seminal questions, previously unasked, about the nature of power. Does power bring order or simply the illusion of order? Can one man's realization of order, achieved through the power he holds, mean in the end simply chaos for the rest of us? May not the man who establishes order-through-power reveal eventually only the chaos in himself? And are the concepts and universals of "order" and "chaos" perhaps not monistic at all, but nominalistic? We may be charged with a new metaphysics of power and order as it pertains to individuals and nations. At least we should be compelled to view the concepts in a new light. As Singh does:

> It has happened in twenty places, twenty countries, islands, colonies, territories—these words with which we play, thinking they are interchangeable and that the use of a particular one alters the truth. I cannot see our predicament as unique. The newspapers even today spell out situations which, changing faces and landscapes, I can think myself into. They talk of the pace of postwar political change. It is not the pace of creation. Nor is it the pace of destruction, as some think. Both these things require time. The pace of events, as I see it, is no more than the pace of a chaos on which strict limits have been imposed. I speak of course of territories like Isabella, set adrift yet not altogether abandoned, where this controlled chaos approximates in the end, after the heady speeches and token deportations, to a continuing order. The chaos lies all within. (p. 230)

If, in the end, we are to see *The Mimic Men* as more than a grand tautological expansion on one man's yearning for and securing "the final emptiness," we must ourselves try to explore beyond Naipaul's insights into questions of order and chaos. His novel is of course only anticipatory of a perspective that time has not yet fully lent us. We are yet to master the patterns of colonial history and the psyches of men— "who have known grandeur beyond the football-pool dreams of [their] neighbors"—who made it, and were changed and defeated by it. We are still caught up, to echo Singh, in the "pace of a chaos." Like him, one must try to "impose order on one's history," but the act must come before falling into sublime and easy simplification. No doubt the strongest lure in a world of flux and complexity is for men to withdraw into their rooms, for nations to withdraw into their corners of the globe, and to discover in an isolation similar to Singh's "order, sequence, regularity." Naipaul warns us away from an illusion so imminently destructive. For once we are no longer willing to fight against Lawrence's idea and Singh's acceptance of "ordered chaos," we are the perfect mimic men; we can become nothing else; for our substance has dissolved into shadow, and that a static one.

IN A FREE STATE: EXILE AND ORDER

IT took Naipaul only a decade to move from his thin, comic ironies about the Caribbean to the refined, if not nearly pure, tragedy of *The Mimic Men*. With it

—the storehouse and culmination of his previous themes—he seemed to have at last solidified his belief in man as an exile, violated by a world first violated by him, and with only a false or imperfect sense of order to redeem his condition. Singh's failure to achieve cultural authenticity (a failure caused as much by his own *hamarteia* as any imperialistic glut), his belated sensitivity to man's inferior place in the natural order, and his hypersensitivity to the inherent shakiness of social and political order were at that time (in 1967) clearly the apogee of Naipaul's tragic vision.

Yet it was just as clear that Singh's race toward shipwreck from one pole to another and his futile attempts to create patterns through "order, sequence and regularity" were recognized by Naipaul as part of a larger, cyclic theory of history that conveyed an even greater sense of futility. Caught up in the order of chaos (a paradox with which the modern world has learned to live comfortably), Singh finds the absolute and terrifying freedom he sought in the final condition of an anonymous exile.

The message of *The Mimic Men* seems supercharged, in defiance of a tone so cool that it often becomes gelid. One would be hard put to find a more apt suggestion of anonymity than Singh's being left—after he has darted behind a pillar to avoid Lady Stella—studying a roomer's attempts to fork a piece of "struggling cheese." Naipaul's choosing to dwell on so trivial a gesture is reserved for a man who no longer can find instruction or meaning elsewhere. Since trifles have all along diverted Singh from "greatness," the irony of situation and tone are perfectly caught. And yet the novel's dying fall, its anticlimax, its near pathos suggest more than Singh's weariness with the "process of life." His—and the book's—last word, "*Dixi*," might just as reasonably have been Naipaul's commentary on the twin themes of exile and order that he had written into all of his works in one way or another, the nihilistic overtones of which had so elaborately resonated in *The Mimic Men* that one hardly expected Naipaul to experiment further in that particular direction. He does, however, with *In a Free State*. For while Naipaul's writing up to that point shows him preoccupied with the ideas of exile and order, *In a Free State* shows him obsessed by them.[1]

The book is dominated by a suggestion that soon takes on the force of a belief. No one is immune from the feeling of not belonging; for exile, in a world geared to uproot each of us at any given moment and fling us pell-mell into uncertitude, can no longer be taken as an intellectual or emotional feeling exclusively nor a conditioned reflex to our disruption, but a congenital defect, as innate to man as his response to heat or cold, his sexual drive, his aggression. Naipaul was now ready to affirm that exile was no longer the final, but the primal condition of man, an archetypal "free state" to be viewed less from chilly heights of abstraction and esthetic distance than to be explored over wider areas of physical encounter, more terrifying, more final, and more pessimistic than he had written about before. After such knowledge, what forgiveness? It was inevitable that this new vision should supersede the old and that Naipaul, in breaking from the security of artistic detachment to broaden his sym-

---

1. I construe this obsession, partly, as being pertinent to the alienated, modern sensibility shared among us all. Though since Naipaul (better than many Englishmen) seems to "fit in" by temperament and intellect to England's Establishment, I am inclined to feel there is a good bit of self-advertisement in his flogging the theme of exile. None of which, of course, undercuts his extraordinary assessment of what it means to be one!

pathies with his characters and engage what was in his own heart, should write his most personal and committed book.

It is true that both these elements are "built in" to *In a Free State* through the extracts from Naipaul's journal, which are the framing prologue and epilogue to the volume. And while it is equally true that Naipaul has elsewhere shown a detachment when writing autobiography as severe as when writing fiction,[2] the "facts" of *In a Free State* cannot help but lend greater truth and conviction to its "fancy." They are there to show how Naipaul's brush with the random "casualties of freedom" (the emigrés, the refugees, the tramp, the desert children) lead to his personal encounter with it and how his growing involvement with exile as a physical certainty (traced by way of his initial aloofness at Piraeus in the prologue to his compulsive intercession at Luxor in the epilogue) breeds the logical commitment to it as that primal condition. They are there to complement the related themes of the stories. Because Naipaul has at last consciously dissolved the shadow line between reality and fiction,[3] they are there to sharpen our own sense of being imprisoned by our culture and our history as we all, exiles to one degree or another, are perpetually adrift "in a free state."

This is the statement at the heart of the book, reached only after Naipaul has done a good deal of stripping and peeling away of the singular illusion harbored by the protagonists in these three linked stories, the illusion that to be in continual exile is

2. In, for example, *The Middle Passage* and *An Area of Darkness*.
3. Or, if I may be permitted to qualify the image with special reference to the first section of this critique, minimized the "blurring of fantasy with reality."

somehow to be continually free. The illusion becomes the prime mover of *In a Free State*, its thrust as well as momentum, and when it is at last dissipated, it accounts for the unavoidable seepage of despair that spreads through the first two pieces to reach floodtide in the title story. Such total despair—a concatenation of fright, bafflement, loneliness, and impotence—is not to be found in *The Mimic Men* even at its gloomiest, and certainly not in *A House for Mr Biswas* or *Mr Stone and the Knights Companion*, for all three are governed by some perception of order, however futile or perverse, however unstable. Now, rather than showing how order or chaos changes and is changed by a life, Naipaul questions their viability to begin with. Can one "in a free state," he asks, in this primal condition of exile really discriminate between chaos and order at all; and if not, what happens to a man when his perceptions of them totally break down?

The one question is at once metaphysical and historic, the other social and cultural. Because Naipaul is wisely aware that no single story contains all the answers, he resorts to a kind of thematic overlapping that allows the second story to reveal something more than the first about the nature of exiles within their free state and allows the final novella to tie together the tryptych as a whole. The technique succeeds almost naturally because of the stories' related themes (a precedent set, in English at least, by *Dubliners*); but its powerful effect depends even more upon a congruent or parallel structure shared among them: the rootless protagonist's movement from an almost supernal innocence to moments of self-doubt and/or disgust when the wellspring of illusion is poisoned, when the past and expectations of the future are annihilated by the "free" act that shatters both will and desire.

* * *

The clearest and undoubtedly least complicated expression of the pattern is to be found in the opening piece, "One out of Many," a comic satire that falls somewhere on the peripheries of *Candide*, Montesquieu's *Lettres persanes*, and *Gulliver's Travels*, though the weary, resigned ending is singularly Naipaul's. What is quite extraordinary is the economy with which Naipaul nudges to the foreground those seemingly gratuitous events, which bring about the decline and fall of Santosh's optimism and push a confused but decent fellow over the edge to despair.

Further, Naipaul's device of letting Santosh narrate the story from his vantage as a new American citizen, living in Washington, D.C., becomes (as in *The Mimic Men*) a self-defining act; but it is not until we discover just how Santosh has come to live in the city, or why, or with whom, that we can also see the technique working to strip him of any of the individuality he had before the desperate assertion of self that ends in the futile stab at complete freedom. On a level that probably needs little analysis at all, the story traces the loss of whatever relative uniqueness Santosh possessed as one out of the many teeming millions in Bombay. Happy among the other "domestics who lived in the street" and respected as the servant of a minor Indian diplomat, he begs to accompany his employer (transferred, with a modest allowance, to Washington) rather than return to his village in the hills. To be "one out of many" in Bombay is, however, much different from being "one out of many" in America where (*e pluribus unum*!) the phrase no longer connotes individuality but consolidation, amalgamation, uniformity, mediocrity at best; and at worst—for a confused and frightened immigrant—displacement and anonymity. Like the thousands of faceless, homogenized Americans who seem to Santosh (privy to their lives through television commercials) "people not quite real [but] people temporarily absent from television," he has become but one more obscurity.

This particular level of the story, I repeat, is immediately graspable, though without some appreciation of its being there one might well overlook the deeper and more disastrous changes that the naive and self-effacing Santosh undergoes. His desire to regain his lost identity in an alien country, coupled with cultural shock, bring about an even fiercer disjunction between what he should feel and what he does, and between what he has come to expect from his thirty-five years in India and what is—at least by American standards—acceptable and real.

On the one hand, such "dissociation of sensibility"—if I may for a moment constrain a famous phrase—lends itself to an art of comic understatement that I imagine Eliot never imagined it could. Santosh, disoriented in thought and feeling, is sequentially overjoyed at being able to bed down in an entire pantry rather than (as in Bombay) in a small cupboard; incredulous at being chased from a cafe because he is barefoot ("Can't you read? We don't serve hippies or bare feet here."); dismayed at having squandered two weeks' pay ($7.50) on refreshments and the movies ("I had been thinking in rupees and paying in dollars"); mystified (at first) that the smell of the "weed" he smokes attracts assorted weirdos (it is of course marijuana); disturbed that a troupe of hippies "chanting Sanskrit words in praise of Lord Krishna" should do so with such an abominable accent and pronunciation;

and appalled and frightened that the *hubshi* (blacks) are "permitted to roam the streets so freely":

> A lot of the *hubshi* were about, very wild-looking some of them, with dark glasses and their hair frizzed out, but it seemed that if you didn't trouble them they didn't attack you. . . .
> . . . I had heard about them in stories and had seen one or two in Bombay. But I had never dreamt that this wild race existed in such numbers in Washington.[4]

This anxiety about the *hubshi* that is soon to turn into a galloping paranoia signals one way in which Naipaul manipulates Santosh's disorientation to gain something other than a comic effect. His chaotic perceptions about life in Washington generate many splendid moments of satire, but the ironies arising from his prejudice against blacks are prodigious: particularly so when they evolve from the sexual ferment set going between Santosh and the large, earthly black chambermaid ("I feared the smells she left behind") bent on seducing him. One irony is that Santosh's prejudice is religious: "It is written in our books, both holy and not so holy, that it is indecent and wrong for a man of our blood to embrace the *hubshi* woman. To be dishonoured in this life, to be born a cat or a monkey or a *hubshi* in the next!" This lends a kind of damning exclusivity to Hinduism, the very tenets of which seek to unite the One with the Many. The attitude is severely ironic, but it is almost as ironic that Santosh's prejudice is a matter of his xenophobia (though it is he, we are reminded again and again, who is the stranger) and his narcissism (the fact of the maid finding him attractive piques his pride to such an extent that, for a while, he compares his features with

---

4. *In a Free State* (London, 1971), pp. 33, 30.

those of every actor on TV). These keystones of Santosh's prejudices are constructs of vanity and innocence more than ignorance and evil, and without them the paradoxes resulting from his sexual escapade would lose a good deal of their force.

Santosh's "fall" (the term is Naipaul's) seems, on the surface at any rate, to be a comic transgression against his ego, his innocence, his prejudice:

> She dragged me down on the couch.... I saw the moment, helplessly, as one of dishonour. I saw her as Kali, goddess of death and destruction, coal-black, with a red tongue and white eyeballs and many powerful arms. I expected her to be wild and fierce; but she added insult to injury by being very playful, as though, because I was small and strange, the act was not real. She laughed all the time. (p. 42)

But in a surprising way the act, however unreal ("it took over and completed itself"), turns out to be the assertion of his freedom; it effects his new identity somewhat like the horrid green suit he buys with money obtained from selling his "weed" and like his discovery that he is now his own man and not a reflection of his employer's "presence." Naipaul caps Santosh's break with his past and thrusts him into "a free state" by timing the one climax with the blacks running amok and burning their neighborhoods. Looking in the mirror, Santosh realizes that he can no longer return to the purity and innocence of his Bombay days, that he can never "become part of someone else's presence again." It is at such a moment—when the chaos without and within has shattered his hold on reality—that he chooses to "escape."

This, I think, constitutes one of the more virulent moments I spoke of above. The illusion of escape soon peters out, and Santosh is thrown back on his own poor devices. The old cycle of dependency and entrapment threatens to begin churning again when he begins working illegally in the restaurant owned by his fellow countryman, now a naturalized American citizen. Though he eventually persuades Priya to pay him nearly ten times his old salary, Santosh finds himself becoming as much a part of the owner's presence as he was of his employer's. Further, his life among the immigrant waiters is calculated on fear, treachery, and jealousy; all of Priya's workers are vying for the "green card" (an American passport) to make them legal, to give them an American identity. The gulf between a green suit and a green card is, as Santosh discovers, immense. Yet once having tasted freedom, Santosh cannot go back; nor, it appears, can he go forward. In the central revelation of the story, Naipaul brings together the whole idea of disorder and unreality that exacts the paradox of self from one "in a free state":

> I had decided to be free, to act for myself. It pained me to think of the exhilaration I had felt during the days of the fire; and I felt mocked when I remembered that in the early days of my escape I had thought I was in charge of myself....
> ... I was good-looking; I had lost my looks. I was a free man; I had lost by freedom.
> ... and I was alone. I hadn't escaped; I had never been free. I had been abandoned. I was like nothing: I had made myself nothing. And I couldn't turn back. (pp. 51, 52, 57)

Had Naipaul attempted to achieve the same sort of effect as in *The Mimic Men*, "One out of Many" might have stopped here, leaving Santosh's attenuated self, like Singh's, suspended in the first throes of anonymity and nihilism. But the upshot of the story—

and its finest irony—is quite different: mainly, I suspect, because the general nature of satire demands some concluding statement about our real and ideal selves and because Santosh's particular problem of freedom pertains to them both.

Objectively Santosh does become free. Naipaul trots out a *dea ex machina*, the black maid, and marries her off to Santosh. In this one masterstroke ("Marry the *hubshi* [Priya advises]. That will automatically make you a citizen. Then you will be a free man"). Santosh accomplishes what he imagined he had wanted all along: She takes him in and he finds shelter; she marries him and he is no longer alone; she makes him a citizen and he is no longer a stranger. The cost for such freedom, a blot on his pride and honor, would seem a small price to pay for one like Santosh who has (quite literally) "come to the end of his rope."

But what Naipaul is really asking is if such a nominal freedom is resolvable through this kind of objectivity. Isn't America, "a free state,"[5] one more chimera raised by chance and accident for the exile? Is not Santosh's quest that of the deluded in search of the illusive? For if the story has told us anything, it is what Santosh can anticipate by becoming, under these strictures, free: identification with blacks that he finds culturally repugnant and who are exiles in their own country; a life where no "television life" awaits him as it does those other Americans who are constantly "cleaning, cleaning, cleaning"; the dark house in which he is forced to live, more occluding than his cupboards; the shutting off of his "mind and heart" to the language, to newspapers and radio, to television, to the

---

5. This *double-entendre* works through all the stories and is one of the more obvious links among them.

films, to the black people who are the only ones who might accept him. In gaining what is apparently his freedom he no longer has anyone to identify with, and without any norm for identification, identity departs with all sense of order and belonging and belief and will. He has become a "presence" to everyone but himself, exiled in flesh and spirit:

> I was once part of the flow, never thinking of myself as a presence. Then I looked in the mirror and decided to be free. All that my freedom has brought me is the knowledge that I have a face and have a body, that I must feed this body and clothe this body for a certain number of years. Then it will be over. (p. 61)

One can scarcely anticipate from the opening of the story this coda of despair, and yet in retrospect it seems anything but unnatural or forced. Like Santosh, we cannot label the particular moment when hope and wonder soured into abjectness and pessimism, for through some insidious synthesis all past moments are continuously being compressed into the present, which, because we fail to fully grasp the process while it is happening, traps us in ignorance and helplessness. More, man's vulnerability as an exile—the freest state that Naipaul can, figuratively or literally, create to coincide with this inability to judge—has fused our perceptions of the two solid forces responsible for our lives, fate and character. To be "in a free state" is thus to be unable to wrest one's character from the ostensible workings of fate or to use circumstances to alter one's character. Man, at least man in exile, consequently moves in a limbo between determinism and existentialism.

* * *

What this does in the darkest spaces of limbo is to raise confusion and disorientation to rage and paralysis, the very progression one finds in "Tell Me Who to Kill." Somehow the maimings in youth of Ralph Singh that bring him to his room in Bayswater are almost simplistic compared to the "endless chain of action" that brings Santosh to *his* dark room in the black section of Washington. Yet even Santosh's final emotions and threat of inaction can only seem dilute when placed beside the grim, warped, defeated personality of the nameless protagonist and narrator of what may be the gloomiest story in the entire Naipaul canon.

For "Tell Me Who to Kill" is not simply a variation on the themes of "One out of Many" but a heightened perversion of them. Idiosyncracies of character have been distorted into obsessions; dishonor has been turned into shame, and shame into a kind of moral defilement; disgust and loathing for oneself and for the human condition are communicated with such intensity that the story could be taken as an extended metaphor of hate; and the hate becomes more self-destructive and tragic because it has been manufactured out of love.

The narrator, an Indian from the West Indies, also ends in a room in London, and, more grimly still, at a wedding party for his only brother, who has married a white. Yet because he, the narrator, is there neither by choice nor chance, but through the blind clash of historic and cultural forces that have effectively reduced him to confusion, he is unable to relieve his obsessions, expiate his shame, disburden himself of hate—even in the most obvious and satisfying way:

> They [the whites] take my money, they spoil my life, they separate us. But you can't kill them. O God, show me the enemy. Once you find out who the enemy is, you can kill him. But these people here they confuse me. Who hurt me? Who spoil my life? Tell me who to beat

back. I work four years to save my money, I work like a donkey night and day. My brother was to be the educated one, the nice one. And this is how it is ending, in this room, eating with these people. Tell me who to kill. (p. 107)

As the story implies, history—the same history at work throughout *The Mimic Men*—is one of the more lethal contributors to the narrator's sense of spoilage and separation. History's formula for the impoverished West Indian who remains in the islands, as for the poor anywhere, is inflexible: omnipresent dirt, stench, sickness, suffering, and an obscure death. Naipaul's twist in this particular story, however, is that the narrator's drive toward the twin goals of escape and freedom is not stimulated by his own ambition, but by that for his brother, Dayo. From that first charged moment when he sees him, a small, smooth, fevered child "lying on the floor on a floursack spread on a sugarsack," he is overcome by the "ambition and shame" to have Dayo succeed, indeed, to suppress his own desires, renounce all thoughts of success for himself to send Dayo to an English university and on to some profession.

The moment, I say, is charged; it is also poignant, and compassionate. Yet as Naipaul knows, and has proved again and again, history is midwife to irony, not to sentimentality. Escaping what he thinks is one order of Necessity, the narrator, as an exile in London, submits to another, and one he can comprehend even less. The pathos of "Tell Me Who to Kill," and its moral tragedy, are something quite different from the descent of character we have witnessed before. Neither the egotism of the little men in the early Caribbean novels, nor the megalomania of Singh, nor the manic depression of Mr. Biswas—all distortions resulting from their obsessive push toward success—is in question here. What is, is the destruction of a psyche brought about through the corruption of pure motives, self-sacrifice, and altruism. Were the narrator white he could fall back, like Mr. Stone, on an affectionate wife, a substantial pension, and a will to possibly create something in the future. But he is "colored." And as I hope to show momentarily, his psyche is not geared to "fall back" on anything at all, since history's upset of order is matched by a brace of cultural deceptions spawned by a Western (and generally Protestant) culture and at odds with the Hindu sensibility.

One of these we have met before in *A House for Mr Biswas*: that plodding ambition and hard work inevitably graft success over stigmas of previous failures. I don't believe it necessary to embark here on a sociological digression to prove how inapplicable the Horatio Alger ethic was to the colonial "coloreds" migrating to England in the 1950s and 1960s and especially to those who had no knowledge at all of the realities of racism and xenophobia. One is not surprised, that is, that the narrator goes bankrupt in his roti-and-curry shop venture within a month, despite his "madness" to succeed.

Yet while his ruin can partially be blamed on "prejudice and regulations," it is also the result of illusions about England nurtured by the many films he has seen in the islands. Such illusions have been responsible for his sending Dayo to London to begin with, so he can become a star-boy like Errol Flim or Fairley Granger or Tyrum Powers or Laurence Oliver, actors whose good looks, sophistication, energy, and accomplishments provide the only analogy for world outside. Naipaul labors neither this, nor the other, cultural hoax, however. For the distortions of appearance —extending in a rather sad way even to the names of the actors themselves—too readily become the solid stuff of reality. When the shadows of the narrator's imagined world dissolve, there is only its shabby substance to confront him, which of course he can no longer face. Reality slips back into dream, and memory into the reality of the ugliness, helplessness, loneliness, and fear he has struggled to avoid, as the last words of the story make painfully clear:

> And now that my brother leave me for good I forget his face already, and I only seeing the rain and the house and the mud, the field at the back with the pará-grass bending down with the rain, the donkey and the smoke from the kitchen, my father in the gallery and my brother in the room on the floor, and that boy opening his mouth to scream, like in *Rope*. (pp. 107–8)

Allusions to this rather grim film have occurred at several points earlier in the story as (one was led to believe) further examples of the narrator's cinematic conditioning. But it is only in its final context that we see that Naipaul means to make of the film something more. *Rope*, one may recall, is about a murder, indeed, a motiveless murder committed by a pair of young intellectuals and psychopaths in order to prove the existence of free will. Perhaps I need but touch on this single aspect of the film for the reader to sense the resonances Naipaul sets going with it and the story, especially in so far as theme and character come into play.

In his desire to give Dayo a good education, to steer him right so he will be successful and free, the narrator exercises his own will to slave away at numerous deadening jobs for money. Again and again he tells us he has "no life of his own": a somewhat melodramatic periphrasis (it would seem) for self-sacrifice and living vicariously through the only person he loves. Melodrama on the surface, one might agree, but a bitter irony always at work beneath. Dayo quite simply is not suited for the role in which the narrator has cast him; nor does he desire to be "free" on his brother's terms. Dayo's freedom comes in eluding his brother's will, in marrying the white girl; though with him go the narrator's will and vicarious existence and desire. Now, objectively, the narrator is himself free, but such freedom is a new sort of death. No one need tell him who to kill, for it is apparent, in the end at least, that he already has done the job:

> I have nowhere to go and I walk now . . . I think how nice it would be if I could just leave it [his curry shop], leave it just like that. . . . If a man could do that, if a man could just leave a life that spoil. . . .
> . . . The life is over. I am like a man who is giving up. I come with nothing, I have nothing, I will leave with nothing. . . .
> . . . And for all this time I am the dead man. (p. 101, 107)

Such confession fixes the narrator at the nadir of mental despair and at the darkest end of Naipaul's line of displaced Westernized Hindus—his mimic men—whose exploratory tilts at power or order or freedom (or all three) end in their too-ready surrender to "nothing." "Tell Me Who to Kill" is not the most detailed treatment of a motif that becomes insistent beginning in *A House for Mr Biswas*, but it is the most concentrated. Because it renders so totally the theme of distortion followed by the destruction of all will and desire, I have reserved comments up till now on why Naipaul plays off theme and motif as he does.

A psychiatrist friend to whom I lent several of Naipaul's novels returned them with a short note saying, in effect, that many of the writer's protagonists who suffered this lack of will power were classic studies of abulia. Like myself, he had been primed on nearly two hundred years of the work ethic (Work, not Truth, shall make ye free!), sixty of Freud and twenty of existentialism; and though he quite acknowledged that sudden exposure to complete freedom probably had something to do with letting the disorder surface, he was not certain *why* the characters should conform so uniformly to a single pattern: unless it were for want of Naipaul's imagination.

My own feelings about the "why" are obviously not allied to the latter suggestion; nor are they dependent upon any of the Western constructs above. To understand the abulia[6] of Mr. Biswas, Ralph Singh, Santosh, and the narrator of "Tell Me Who to Kill," one must understand a bit about the Hindu's priming and about several tenets of Hinduism itself as they relate directly to the "free state" which, in its turn, is connected with that stoic negatavism Naipaul's characters so readily seem to adopt.

Let me quote, first of all, from a popular book on Hinduism, just enough summary to show how striking this connection is:

> Hinduism ... may be characterized as a system of the means appropriate for the attainment of Liberation. ... The nonliberated man is subject to common destiny: enslaved by his actions which follow him indefinitely ... he is condemned to be reborn; and as most human

---

6. By "abulia" I am referring to the concepts of renunciation, annihilation, nihilism, etc., that I have used throughout this critique. The esthetic or critical value of any psychological label is, needless to say, suspect.

actions are tainted by malice, the risk of being reborn in a lower condition, ultimately as an animal, is greater than the possibility of achieving an exalted state. *Karman* (consequence of action) and *saṃsāra* (indefinite transmigration of living beings) . . . are postulates based on a conviction which is not open to discussion. Existence (life) flows as a torrent; man suffers passively the necessity of death in order that he be born and die, again and again. This is the basis of Indian pessimism . . . But there is an essential corollary: by his actions man can, to a certain extent, direct his destiny. . . . . Evidently, however, it would be still better to cease to act at all, to exhaust all the reserves of *karman*. Hence the prime importance of renunciation, the inherent negativism of Indian experience.[7]

This cessation of activity and exhaustion of reserves seem to be precisely the Naipauline experience we have been considering; and one can see how very un-Western it is; indeed, how very un-Judaeo-Christian, if I may interpolate yet another of our constructs as well. Naipaul's Hindu does not, like his ascetic Christian counterpart, give up life to find life; he does not die, either literally or metaphorically, to be reborn. Quite the contrary. His "renunciation" brings about a liberation well outside the salvation concept of Christian eschatology, mainly because the freeing process takes place in this world and not the next. To the Hindu liberation, or *mokṣa* as it is called, is the release from the necessity of being reborn; and knowing this should make his obsessional coveting of the "free state" much less mystifying.

For at least one of the two thousand years of Christianity, our social activity has proved glaringly at odds with our religion and ethics. Such conflicts scarce-

---

7. *Hinduism*, edited by Louis Renou (New York, 1962), pp. 43–44.

ly exist in Hinduism, for all phases of human activity are of a piece. *Dharma* (moral activity), *artha* (interested activity), and *kāma* (playful activity) are wound up to be released in the final and fourth phase, *moksa*: the moment when one is liberated from the will or desire for any further activity whatsoever. In one way, then, the freedom achieved by Naipaul's protagonists is a necessary and almost inescapable result of the four-fold process. They are no longer required to order their lives, for they have acknowledged that life has no order. Order, for that matter, means continual enslavement to the cycle, and a man would only be foolish to willingly remain a slave. When activity is suspended, however, the cycle is broken, and freedom, uprooting and chaotic, comes at last. In another way, such freedom is simply a dead end. The paradoxes that emerge from *being* "in a free state," Naipaul implies, can be no less awesome than those that grow out of *attaining* it.

Let me say at this point that I should be thought obtuse if I seriously thought my explanation of the "why" of all this could possibly console Santosh or the narrator of "Tell Me Who to Kill." Whether one is the victim of a Vedic heritage or the incarnation of a psychological tag, does not make the ironies of existence any less grim. Naipaul has proved immensely thoughtful (as well as novelistically clever) in showing how *moksa* and abulia may be heads and tails of the same coin. But does one state or the other carry beyond the inherent flaw that fated the condition to begin with?

I am of course asking how "universal" Naipaul means these two stories to be and how universally the reader may be expected to take them. Naipaul's Hindus are model exponents—within limits—for his theme of exile and order; yet they *are* outsiders; furthermore, they never imagine themselves anything else. And I suspect that a liberal, intellectual Westerner, however sensitive to the hate and insecurity spawned by racism, the degrading boundaries imposed by poor education, and the despair generated by cultural alienation, must empathize with these outsiders at some distance only: the same distance, perhaps, that Naipaul keeps from the refugees on the "dingy little Greek steamer," and from the hounded and terrified tramp at Piraeus:

> [He] was standing there alone . . . exposed to the cold wind and the smut from the smokestack. . . . How fragile that face was, worked over by distress; . . . he looked close to tears. It was strange. He looked for company but needed solitude; he looked for attention, and at the same time wanted not to be noticed.
> I didn't disturb him. I feared to be involved with him.
> (pp. 13–14)

"Involved" is the key word here, and up until the title story of the volume, the exiles' alternatives have been pretty well glossed. In the prologue, Naipaul, *in propria persona*, plays the part of the outsider who shuns involvement; Santosh and the West Indian narrator are outsiders who cannot help theirs; the author appears immune to the virulence suffered by his protagonists. Yet there is a third alternative. What of the outsider, in self-imposed exile, who believes he belongs, who believes he has found freedom in transplantation to an alien culture? The stripping away of such an illusion and the breakdown of such a man should, I think, still any remaining doubts of the volume's universality. There would seem scant hope in finding a "place" or a "home" in the world if the most fixed convictions of belonging, the most tenacious and voluntary commitment to order, the most heartfelt aspirations to freedom are so capriciously and matter-of-factly massacred.

* * *

The first of these conditions immediately distinguishes "In a Free State" from the preceding stories. Bobby, the young, homosexual British administrative officer who once had a "breakdown" at Oxford, has found physical and mental fulfillment in Africa. For him, Africa is "the empty spaces, the safe adventure of long fatiguing drives on open roads, the other Africans, boys built like men." His accomplished importunings in pidgin English of "rough trade" (as pick-ups among homosexuals are called) have opened doors to sexual indulgence that a careerist civil servant would scarcely find possible, or desirable, in dear old constricted England. For a shilling he can hold hands; for five shillings he can generally do more.

Yet the effortlessness and casualness of such promiscuity, as well as its nature, free it from "mockery and self-disgust." It is a mark of Bobby's liberation, and that he can solicit blacks in bars, on the road, and elsewhere is also a mark of theirs. In its own way, Bobby's connecting with the Africans is less corrupting than the pukkah and colonial mentality (one has read about it in Forster and Orwell and it has not changed much since) that does not connect at all. Bobby is a trifle solemn and a bit of an ass, but as Naipaul is at pains to show, he is also a man of goodwill, an innocent, and a romantic who draws from Africa feelings of exhilaration and renewal similar to those experienced by the first American settlers in the West, but without their attendant fears. Bobby, wrapped in a cocoon of safety spun out of white privilege and his own "rules," has no fears. Any he did have were left behind in England where, during his long breakdown, he saw himself "becoming a ghost." "Africa saved my life," he tells Linda, one of the wives from the government compound, early on in their trip. And it is here his life now is.

Such confessions could have come off as dreary and lugubrious had Naipaul not set his tone through the characters, but rather the other way round. As he works them, however, the guarded preliminaries between Bobby and Linda are as innocuous and real as they should be with two people who share a "half-relationship" based on "uncertainty rather than suspicion," which is not to suggest the absence of some other underlying mood. The atmosphere Naipaul creates through their game chit-chat, their forced and actual cheerfulness, the gossip about the English and Africans they know mutually, and the banal exchanges of small confidences is of that suppressed calm only a hairsbreadth away from tension. Accommodating Linda by agreeing to drive her from the capital of the "Southern Collectorate" to the foreigners' compound some distance away—and the action of the novel comprises little more than their adventures along the route—has effectively disrupted Bobby's chances for pickups. Linda, too, is overpoweringly a woman, with a reputation for being a "man-eater" as well. And she is also a confessed outsider who anticipates joining the "white exodus" south—that is to South Africa—with her husband. Bobby seems to be, in the most important way, what Linda is not. He is genuinely posessed by the country; he is (so he imagines) a part of it; and he has found (so he thinks) an inviolable place in it. I have not employed these parentheses to play coy, for the ironies both of motive and intention are implicit in the text. Bobby's sober statements about belonging to Africa and Africa belonging to him, while not signs of arrogance, do reflect the slightest feelings of his superiority to Linda. Yet such overprotestations might just as easily be the old insecurity reasserting itself: a whistling-in-the-dark on the dark continent. The ambiguity, though, is part of Naipaul's maneuvering Bobby into the theme. One properly senses even at this point in the story that Bobby's grim earnestness brands him as somewhat vulnerable. That hairsbreadth between calm and tension is identical to the one between defensive and defenseless, and both of the ordered terms in the sets are presently to break down into their disordered counterparts.

In these brief bits of thought and talk, Bobby and Linda foreshadow responses to what later happens to them, and I hope this fact will excuse what seems my undue concern with a short movement in the longer symphony of disintegration. By "responses" I am thinking of more than their reactions to the discomfort, mental lacerations, and physical humiliations they experience on the road to the compound, though there would appear to be enough here for several novellas at least. What I am thinking of are the combined responses of them and the reader and the novelist to the entropy in which Bobby's (and to a lesser degree Linda's) breakdown plays a small part. Naipaul builds up Bobby's false trust in this African Eden, in this achieved and ordered world merely to trace its erosion: an erosion that begins as suddenly, progresses as relentlessly, and ends as violently as the rain hammering on their car for most of the drive and muddying the road. Yet Bobby and Linda's personal reversals and mounting panic are, like the natural disasters, only the rolling foreground of a picture juxtaposing Africa's man-made catastrophes against its chaotic history; and this, in a literal as well as symbolic way, is bound up with exile.

Naipaul gets at some of the larger patterns of the theme in the very opening paragraph:

> In this country in Africa there was a president and there was also a king. They belonged to different tribes. The enmity of the tribes was old, and with independence their anxieties about one another became acute. The king and the president intrigued with the local representatives of white governments. The white men who were appealed to liked the king personally. But the president was stronger; the new army was wholly his, of his tribe; and the white men decided that the president was to be supported. So that at last, this weekend, the president was able to send his army against the king's people. (p. 111)

The historic setting is hardly new; it is indeed almost cliché. We have been there before, countless of times in the fifties and sixties, elsewhere as well as in Africa: a *coup d'état* is in the making "in a free (!) state." Yet once we are keyed in to Naipaul's theme, the cast of his prose seems to go beyond spare understatement and reportage to something fabulistic, even allegorical. Because of its emphasis on the anonymity of king, country, president, the passage depicts a condition not merely historically typical but archetypical: man's sudden uprooting from (shaky) stability and his topple into disorder. What exacerbates the condition and makes Naipaul's mythic overlay—which, I grant, must be inferred from his style—of immense significance is that this time the chaos has been generated from within. And how likely a refuge for belonging and order is such a country to prove? The ousted insider, the king, is, we learn later on, being hunted by presidential troops and is trying to get out of the country and into exile before he is murdered. The main roads, growing progressively impassable because of the rain and mud, have further been blockaded, and it is unfortunately such a main road that Bobby and Linda must travel to reach their compound, which, also unfortunately, is in the territory of the king's people.

The reason Bobby and Linda leave the capital's relative safety to drive several hundred miles through a country engaged in civil war is a matter of simple ignorance: No signs of the crisis have yet appeared in "the colonial city, with colonial glamour." This unawareness is a fine touch and the premise basic to any study charting colonial retreat: The white colonial mentality always does seem ignorant of the forces working to undermine and reject it. Such obliviousness puts Bobby's faith in having caught the temper and tempo of the country, and his affect for the Africans in a different light. He is totally unprepared for what is to happen; nor has he the foggiest notion of how he shortly is to become caught up in the chaos confirmed by historic precedent. The best Naipaul can do for Bobby is provide him with an ironic intuition of chaos and order together, ironic because it suggests Bobby's —and our—effete reliance on any token sign of order spelling out civilization:

> On the other bank tree trunks were black in the gloom; leaves and branches hung low. The wood of a fairy-tale, far from home: what was so recently man-made, after the forests had been cut down and the forest-dwellers flushed out and dismissed, what had perhaps been intended only as an effect of art in a landscape made

secure, had become natural. It spoke of an absence of men, danger. (p. 139)

I call attention to this particular revelation because no other moment in the novel fixes so perfectly Bobby's confidence in men; yet no other so well prepares for the crushing of this obstinate illusion in the vise of irony gradually tightening with each sinuous turn of the road. The natives, freed by the technicians of colonialism and civilization from their natural savagery, are the very ones that go furthest to depriving Bobby of dignity, mocking his authority, shattering his sense of decency, and limiting his freedom. The closer he and Linda come to the safety of the compound, the more severe (and tangible) become the scars inflicted upon them by the Africans, and the more they feel useless, alone, exiled.

Their long car trip, beginning casually, half-heartedly even to develop—especially for Bobby—into a nightmare, makes a rather instructive parallel with "Heart of Darkness." To the modern sensibility, Conrad's tale is the first, and perhaps still the best example of the quest as night-sea journey, of the travelogue as *Bildungsroman*. Marlow finds Kurtz and discovers himself. His penetration into the heart of the many hearts of darkness is a burrowing into the moral corruption gnawing away at any colonial power founded on egotism and materialism, but it is also Conrad's method of affirming that the worst (Kurtz) is but a corruption of the best; that civilization and order are preferable to savagery and chaos; and that, in the long run, the white race has the know-how to light up the dark places with civilization's torch. Yet it is the darkness, the sensual luxuriance, the fascination for the primitive and inchoate, the chaos, savagery and perversions that always make the most forceful impressions on one on rereading the novella. The power of "Heart of Darkness" is in its jungle scenario. It is one of genius's most magnificent successes at making the pathetic fallacy dwarf even a character of Kurtz's mythic dimensions. In the end, we do not admire order so much as fear disorder.

"In a Free State" stimulates an identical negative reaction, though Bobby's journey (literally and imagistically) is into the light and is beset not by the pathetic but the human fallacy: namely, that whites can ever be free of guilt or fear so long as they are, to the blacks, apostles of order. Unlike Marlow, Bobby after his experiences cannot bring back a "lie" to the orderly world of the English compound, for civilization—white civilization—cannot be protected from "the horror" that is itself. Bobby (in our last glimpse of him) must suffer the lie silently, alone; his only recourse is to sack Luke, his houseboy; feel frustrated; resign himself to leave. Naipaul's vision is much more desolate and final than Conrad's. I would call it Spenglerian in that Naipaul sees the self-assertion of the Africans paralleled by the disintegration of the English. Marlow—and Conrad—would have liked to believe that what "redeems" the principle of conquest and colonialization "is the idea only." For Naipaul, as well as for students of history, that idea was a mere dream, too soon and too irrevocably become nightmare. In a very real way it is this sort of nightmare Bobby experiences; though his movements toward it also become an allegory on the decline and fall of British colonialism, as its initial phase of toleration and paternalism gave way to haughtiness and insecurity, and that, finally, to panic and retreat.

The stages leading to Bobby's personal nightmare are hardly as convoluted as the historic cycles they appear to parallel; but they are as artfully constructed as a ship in a bottle. Each incident along the way reflects a shift in Bobby's attitude toward Africa, in Bobby and Linda's attitudes toward each other and of course in Bobby's attitude toward himself. And all the shifts, I might add, are linked to the climax of the novella in which Bobby is teased, mocked, baited, roughed-up, and then beaten by the African soldiers. Naipaul means such incidents to grind forward from lower to higher gear, to show how Bobby, through his second breakdown, once more becomes a "ghost," and to effect the final turn of the screw—the massacring of Bobby's last illusion about freedom and Africa—through an accretion of lesser turns. What one must notice about all these encounters is the increasing violence associated with them. As Bobby and Linda draw nearer to the "safety" of the English compound, they fall prey more easily to the dangers outside it. In a "free state," in exile, those most susceptible to order become the most vulnerable to chaos. This concept is neither ironic nor paradoxical. What is, though, is Bobby's knowledge that safety—if it is possible be safe in the world—must be sought through restraint rather than freedom; he cannot shed his identity as a white nor as an Englishman. We are back once more in Naipaul's singular world where the obsession with freedom ends in claustrophobic entrapment. Grubby Miguel Street, Singh's seedy rooms, Mr. Biswas' house, the English compound are all microcosms holding an identical truth in suspension: One may be free, one may be safe, but one cannot be both.

Bobby's beating is the dramatic culmination of

this truth, but Naipaul forshadows the game's ending midway in the journey: in the perfectly conceived interlude at the colonel's unfrequented and nearly abandoned hotel in the small resort town. The scenes crystallize what has gone before and anticipate what is to come. Here, the superfluousness and dysfunction of the colonial—a condition fated soon to be Bobby's own—implies that chaos may be no more than order recoiling on itself. The implications are everywhere: in the architecture of the anachronistic hotel, in the stinking brown water limping from ornate fixtures, in the rotting vegetation of the lake, in the once domesticated dogs (trained by the colonials to attack the Africans) now gone wild and roaming the town in packs, in the colonel's life sustained by the "hate" he bears his African servants. Though as he tells Bobby, it is not really "hate" at all:

> "They say there's good and bad everywhere. There's no good and bad here. They're just Africans. They do what they have to do. That's what you have to tell yourself. You can't hate them. You can't even get angry with them. Really angry." (p. 193)

More than a blunt diagnostician of African amorality, the colonel, with his settler mentality and reactionary disengagement, is a relic of that most civilized of chauvinists, the British colonial, whose own home-grown morality was responsible for the lack of empathy (rather than actual antipathy) toward the colonies' natives, and for the poor judgment (rather than actual stupidity) in the matter of colonial affairs: both of which are deficiencies that drove the last nails in the coffin of the Empire. Orwell's "Shooting an Elephant" is still probably the best single document on colonial paranoia and on the Englishman's insane need to place moral constructions on the native's every action and to impute some corresponding hostile motive to every action that goes against this morality. In a sense, such conditioning, which even Oxonian homosexuals are unable to escape, allows Bobby to magnify the impertinences of the two African hitchhikers and the carelessness of the African gas station attendant beyond all reasonable proportion and to set himself up for the subsequent encounter with insult and physical violence. There is a strange and mocking justice in this, for it is as inevitable as Bobby's outburst at Linda that takes the form of violent verbal insult, after his animosity has built during the trip.

> "There are so many like you, Linda. We musn't let our minds grow rusty. We are among savages and we need our cultural activities. We are among these very dirty savages and we must remind ourselves that we have this loveliness. Do we use our vaginal deodorant daily? . . .
>
> "*Do we? Do We?* What brand do we use? Hot Girl, Cool Girl, Fresh Girl? Girl-Fresh? You're nothing. You're nothing but rotting cunt. There are millions like you, millions, and there will be millions more. . . .
>
> "There are millions like you. And millions like Martin. You are *nothing*." (p. 226)

Naipaul gets a good deal of mileage out of Bobby and Linda's swapping confidences and half-truths, but quite clearly the exchanges are directed toward this one explosive turn where Bobby signals his loss of control. It is his ugliest moment; yet though he strips himself of all dignity and civilization to rage on like a vicious, frustrated, impotent "queen," it must also be called, I suppose, his most tragic. We are in at the near total breakdown of a very sick and troubled mind that at the last shift tries to assert itself through the aggression and cruelty it abhors. And so Bobby's beating should neither appall us nor strike us as a gratuitous bit of theatrics. It is the physical counterpart to his previous, self-inflicted mental drubbing. First Bobby's illusions are battered and crushed like the myriad white butterflies that come out of the forest "like flakes of snow"; then a piece of Bobby himself is broken.

The violence of the soldiers against Bobby is, alas, the one real experience he will take away from Africa —and we are fairly certain he will leave, though not immediately, but imminently and bitterly:

> Then he felt the boot hard on his right wrist, and he could have cried then, at the clear pure pain, the knowledge of the fracture, so deliberate, the knowledge that what had been whole all his life had been broken.
> (p. 239)

Here, the one calculated, "deliberate," free act of a moment cancels out whatever identity Bobby had ploddingly built up in his freedom and exile over the years and shatters the hope for anything more like it in the future. But Naipaul shows more than the brutal annihilation of a single dream. Bobby must bear the weight—perhaps too heavily—of whatever poetic justice Naipaul sees attending the colonial disaster in general. Bobby, the true nature of his exile defined precisely at the instant the fat soldier's boot fractures his wrist, changes from casual victim to scapegoat. The purity of a vision is displaced by the purity of a pain at once real and symbolic. He is "humiliated, denuded, disfigured," but what is done to him is no more or no less than what any colonial power throughout its tenure has done to others. For Bobby is shattered to realize that Africa no longer wants him, that he does not belong, that he is not free. Yet worse is the unconscious (suppressed, if one prefers) acknowledgment that goes along with the realization: that he, like Linda, like the British in the compound, and like those hundreds of exiles who thought to live free and safe and ordered amidst chaos and change, may be simply nothing!

* * *

The final paradox posed in *In a Free State* is not, however, lodged in fiction but in fact, and it adds a further dimension to everything Naipaul has written to date.

It comes in initially by way of a vignette found in the volume's "Epilogue, From a Journal." Lunching at Luxor in Egypt, Naipaul watches some grubby desert children scramble in the sand for bits of food thrown by a group of Italian tourists. As they scramble, they are beaten off by a man with a camel-whip, who cracks it near, then on them. To the Italians, to the other tourists of assorted nationalities, to the man with the camel-whip, even to the children—to everyone, that is, except to the indignant Naipaul, this gratuitous display of cruelty is a game, interrupted only when the author walks over to the man, takes away his whip, and throws it in the sand. Performed cooly, but with "anxiety," the gesture leaves Naipaul feeling "exposed and futile." He retreats to his table and lapses into indifference, knowing the children will soon return to rake through the sand for the food, and knowing the same game will be reenacted when the next package tour passes through.

But indeed is it "indifference" at all? The Naipaul of the epilogue is scarcely the same Naipaul of the prologue who stood by and watched the frightened tramp being bullied and persecuted. He does not intercede at Piraeus; he does at Luxor. He chooses to become involved, though momentarily, in the small violations of the outcasts and oppressed. In those few moments of truth, Naipaul concentrates the confusion of Santosh, the repulsion of the narrator of "Tell Me Who to Kill," the humiliation and denudation of Bobby, but he chooses to act rather than be acted upon. It is a noble display, and a rare confession. Naipaul—lucid, logical, removed, seemingly resistant—surrenders to the disorderly feelings that shatter both the dispassion and detachment of novelist and exile. His response out of "anger and a sense of injustice" separates him from the lookers-on who would play the "game." Yet this humanitarian act catches him in the paradoxical toils hitherto reserved for his fictions only. When our meticulously conceived and compulsively nurtured sense of order breaks down, as it must when at odds with the scheme of things, we are left vulnerable and exposed. Naipaul, then, is hardly indifferent. Seldom can we find a novelist so openly linking arms with his protagonists nor converting poetic justice into a current truth about the human condition.

Naipaul's answers to why paradoxes arise from something so apparently solid and rooted as one's sense of order allow little room for rejoicing, though as I mentioned at the outset of this critique, Naipaul is not noted for being a cheery writer. What the answers should do is make us aware of the contradictions—both true and absurd—that are fundamental to any idea of order that pretends to be pure. We are, whether we care to admit it or not, pawns in the great chaotic shifts of history, or actors rehearsing daily small tragicomedies of chaos; and with these limitations in mind we should recognize the dangers of impressing a pure idea of order on these large and small stagings. Only during one brief epoch in the thousands of years of our civilization, Naipaul reflects, might so singular a unity of being have existed:

> Perhaps that had been the only pure time, at the beginning, when the ancient artist, knowing no other land, had learned to look at his own and had seen it as complete. But it was hard, travelling back to Cairo, looking with my stranger's eye at the fields and the people who worked in them, the dusty towns, the agitated peasant crowds at railway stations, it was hard to believe that there had been such innocence. Perhaps that vision of the land, in which the Nile was only water, a blue-green chevron, had always been a fabrication, a cause for yearning, something for the tomb. (pp. 255–56)

Naipaul is not optimistic; yet he is, in his curious way, hopeful. He hints at the integrity and innocence man once had, and he acknowledges their loss, but only to free us from our own obstinate illusions about how the world should be. Like purity, order may be an illusion; and as the impure action might do some good in an impure world, so our glimpses into chaos may mature that vision of order with which we ultimately can live. In annihilating such illusions, Naipaul makes the vision seem possible.